Key Data

1996 edition

Production Co-ordinator: PHIL LEWIN

Production Team: ANDY LEACH
ANGELA CANNELL

Statistical Advisor: CAROL SUMMERFIELD

London: HMSO

Contents

		Page
	Introduction	4
1	**Geography** Standard regions and counties of England and Wales. Local authority regions of Scotland and Boards of Northern Ireland.	5
2	**Population & vital statistics** Resident population, population change, age and gender, ethnic group and age, conceptions, births, deaths, marriages, divorces.	7
3	**Employment** Labour force, economic activity status of mothers, women in employment, unemployment rates, economic activity rates, temporary employees, employees receiving job-related training, redundancy rates by occupation.	13
4	**National accounts** Gross national and domestic product, GDP income and expenditure, index numbers of output.	19
5	**UK finance** Monetary aggregates, PSBR, interest and exchange rates and security prices, building society and bank transactions, consumer credit.	27
6	**Balance of payments** Current account, transactions in UK external assets and liabilities.	31
7	**European Community** Regions, comparisons, migration, comparative purchasing power of the pound, domestic energy consumption, average hours worked, prison population.	35
8	**Prices** Retail Prices Index, Tax and Price Index, household expenditure, consumers' expenditure, net lending to consumers, consumer credit, household saving.	45
9	**Incomes** Household income, pensioners' gross income, average weekly and hourly earnings, gross weekly earnings by gender, age and selected occupation, income paid and redistributed through taxes and benefits, household disposable income.	51

10 **Crime & justice**   57

Recorded offences, offenders found guilty and sentenced for indictable offences, victims of crime by ethnic group, clear-up rates, criminal supervision orders, prison population, receptions under sentence, sentence length, complaints against the police.

11 **Environment**   63

Recycling levels, air pollutants, water quality of rivers and canals, fish stocks, abstractions, production of primary fuels.

12 **Transport**   67

Purpose of, estimated passenger kilometres, motor vehicles licensed, index numbers of road traffic, households with use of a car, bus and rail journeys, port and airport arrivals, international passenger movements, casualty and death rates.

13 **Lifestyles & tourism**   73

Time use, household tasks, leisure activities, radio listening, newspapers and magazine reading, participation in leisure activities, holidays, travel and tourism.

14 **Education**   79

Adult literacy and numeracy standards, pupils reaching expected standards, qualifications attained by gender, NVQ targets, pupils by type of school, class sizes, enrolments in further and higher education, destination of first degree graduates.

15 **Health & personal social services**   85

Life expectation by gender and age, cardiovascular diseases, alcohol consumption, cigarette smoking, breast cancer screening, AIDS cases, NHS waiting lists, staffing, expenditure on the NHS, children looked after by local authorities, social services for elderly people.

16 **Housing**   91

Stock, indicators of investment and prices of dwellings, new mortgages by gender, repossessions, types of dwelling.

17 **Energy**   95

Inland energy consumption, coal supply, use and stocks, natural gas production and supply, electricity production, delivery of petroleum products.

18 **Index**   99

Introduction

Welcome to the 1996 edition of *Key Data*. The aim of this publication is to present you with basic statistics in the main economic and social areas. This year the content has been entirely revised and a new chapter focusing on the environment added.

The tables selected for reproduction have been taken directly from other publications, most of which are also produced by the Office for National Statistics:

- **Annual Abstract of Statistics**
- **Regional Trends**
- **Social Trends**
- **Social Focus on Women**
- **Economic Trends**
- **United Kingdom Economic Accounts**
- **United Kingdom Balance of Payments (The 'Pink Book')**
- **Monthly Digest of Statistics**

The original publication is named under each reproduced table or chart, whilst within the table or chart there is normally a reference to the source of the figures.

With this variety of origins it is inevitable that the tables do not always conform to a standard presentation. Nevertheless they have in common that they relate to the United Kingdom in total unless clearly stated otherwise, that figures for less than a year are seasonally adjusted unless stated otherwise, and that where symbols are used they have the following meanings:

-	*nil*
..	*not available*
italics	*normally indicate percentages*
*	*average (or total) of five weeks*
†	*revised figure*

If you have any comments about the publication, please write to the Key Data Co-ordinator, Marketing and Customer Service Division, Office for National Statistics, Room 60a/3, Government Buildings, Great George Street, London, SW1P 3AQ.

If you require further information about the statistics included in this publication, please contact the source department listed at the foot of the relevant table. Contact details are available from the ONS enquiry service on 0171-270 6363/6364 or from the publication *Government Statistics - a Brief Guide to Sources* which provides a list of the most important government statistical publications and contact points. This is available free from the ONS library in Newport; telephone 01633 812973.

ONS Databank

The ONS Databank provides a wide range of data on disk, including many series from this publication. For more details about the availability of datasets, prices, or to place your order, please telephone, write or fax: Sales Office, Office for National Statistics, Room 131/4, Government Buildings, Great George Street, London SW1P 3AQ. Telephone 0171-270 6081 or fax 0171-270 4986. The ONS does not currently offer direct on-line access for these data but a list of host bureaux offering such a facility is available on request from the ONS.

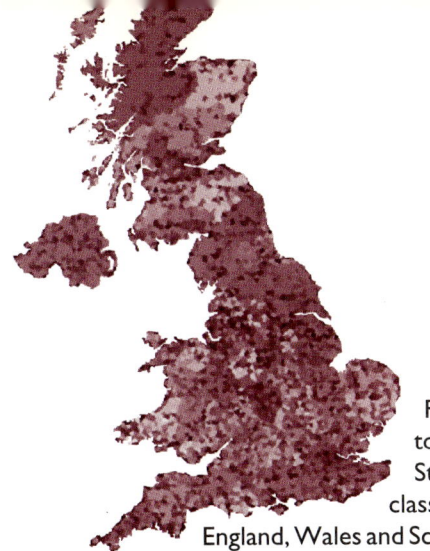

one

Geography

Definitions and sources

For statistical purposes, England is divided into eight regions, and these together with Wales, Scotland and Northern Ireland are known as the Standard Regions of the United Kingdom. These Standard Regions are also classified as level 1 regions for the purposes of the European Community. England, Wales and Scotland together form Great Britain. The Isle of Man and the Channel Islands are not part of Great Britain/United Kingdom.

On 1 April 1996, single tier councils - known as Unitary Authorities - replaced the current two tier system of Counties and Local Authority Districts (LADs) in Wales and Regions and LADs in Scotland. The maps below and overleaf for these countries are therefore valid only up to that date.

1.1 Standard regions and counties of England and Wales

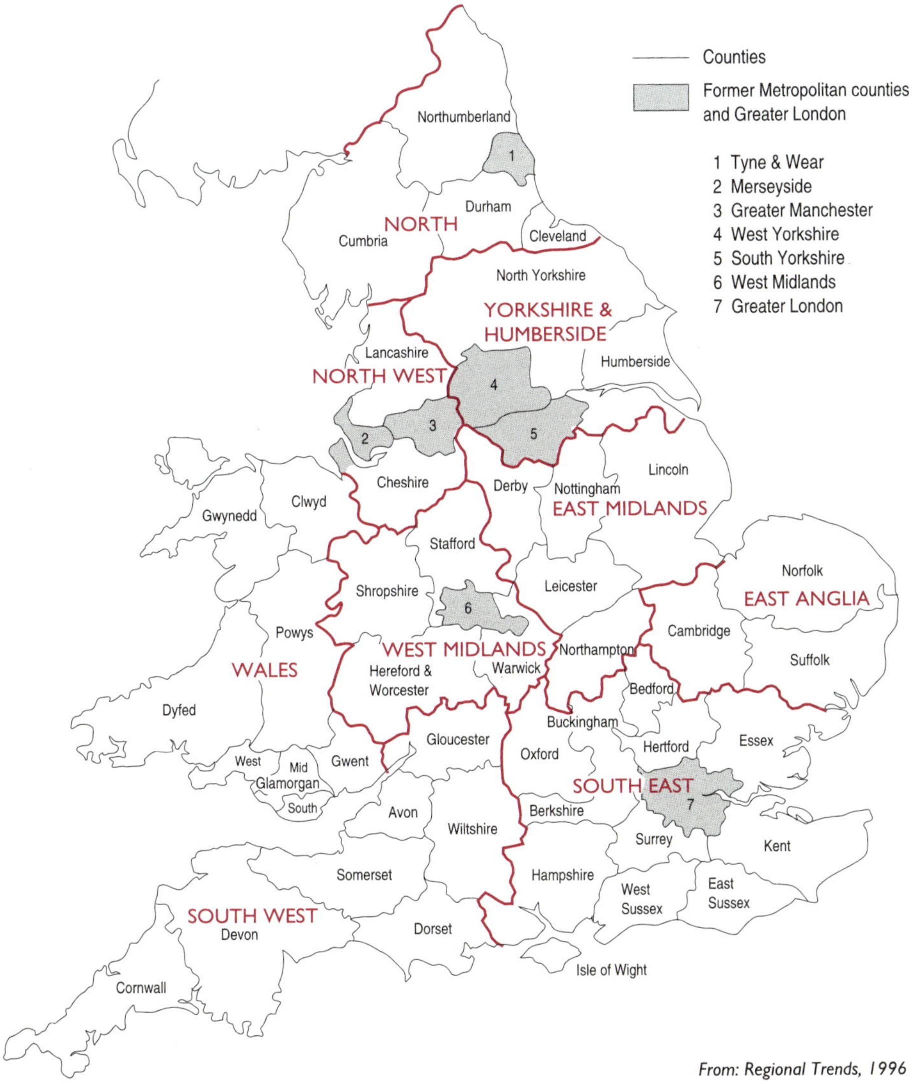

—— Counties

▨ Former Metropolitan counties and Greater London

1 Tyne & Wear
2 Merseyside
3 Greater Manchester
4 West Yorkshire
5 South Yorkshire
6 West Midlands
7 Greater London

From: Regional Trends, 1996

1.2 Local Authority regions of Scotland and Boards[1] of Northern Ireland

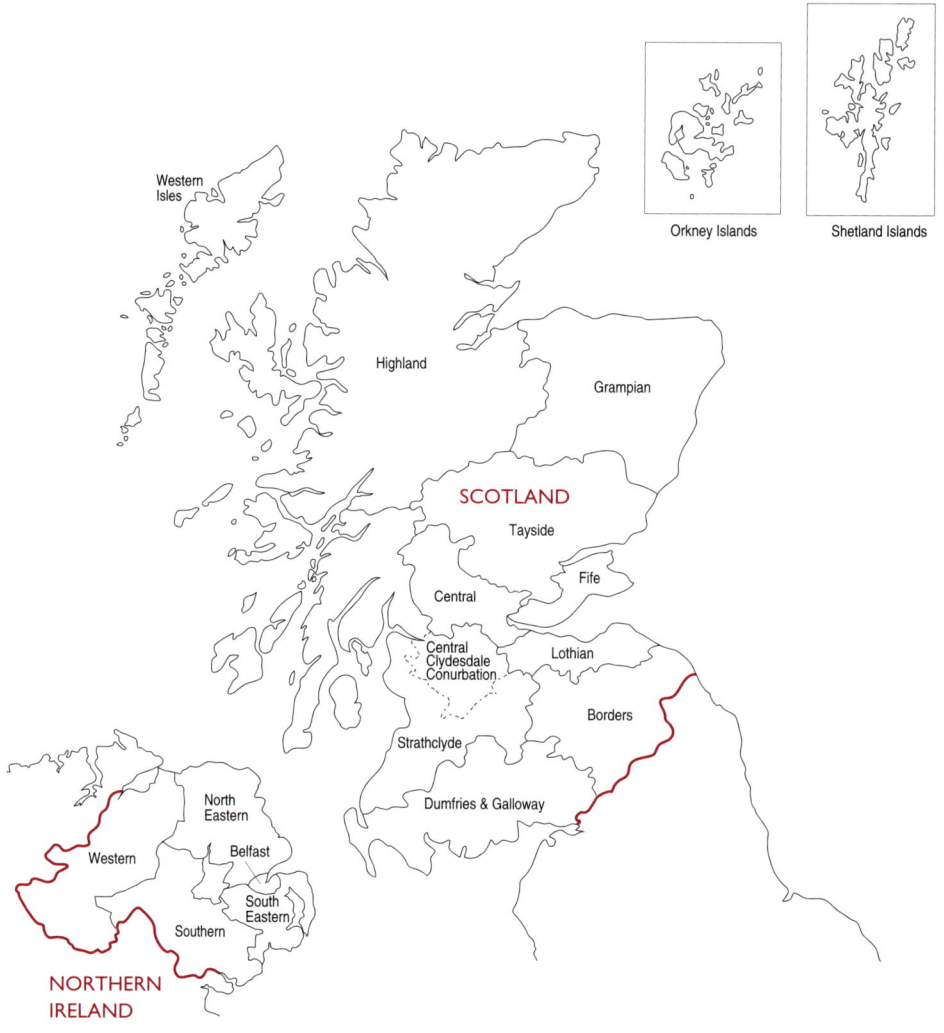

Orkney Islands   Shetland Islands

Western Isles

Highland

Grampian

SCOTLAND

Tayside

Fife

Central

Central Clydesdale Conurbation

Lothian

Borders

Strathclyde

Dumfries & Galloway

North Eastern

Western

Belfast

South Eastern

Southern

NORTHERN IRELAND

1 Education and Library Boards. For Health and Social Services Boards and travel-to-work areas see *Regional Trends* Appendix.

From: Regional Trends, 1996

two

Population & vital statistics

Definition of resident population

The estimated resident population of an area includes all those usually resident in the area, whatever their nationality. Members of HM Forces stationed outside the United Kingdom are excluded. Students are taken to be resident at their term-time addresses.

Figures for the United Kingdom do not include the population of the Channel Islands or the Isle of Man.

The population estimates for mid-1991 onwards are final figures based on the 1991 Census of Population with allowance for subsequent births, deaths and migration. Population estimates for the years 1982-1990 have been revised, to give a smooth series consistent with both 1981 and 1991 Census results.

For other sources see: *Guide to Official Statistics, 1996 edition* (520 pages approximately, fully indexed) HMSO.

2.1 Mid-year estimates of resident population[1]

	England and Wales			Scotland			Northern Ireland			United Kingdom		
	Males	Females	Persons	Males	Females	Persons	Males	Females	Persons	Males	Females	Persons
1980	24 156	25 448	49 603	2 501	2 693	5 194	755	778	1 533	27 411	28 919	56 330
1981	24 160	25 474	49 634	2 495	2 685	5 180	754	783	1 538	27 409	28 943	56 352
1982	24 148	25 466	49 613	2 490	2 677	5 167	754	784	1 538	27 391	28 927	56 318
1983	24 190	25 491	49 681	2 484	2 669	5 153	756	788	1 543	27 429	28 948	56 377
1984	24 270	25 540	49 810	2 482	2 664	5 146	760	791	1 550	27 511	28 995	56 506
1985	24 369	25 621	49 990	2 479	2 658	5 137	763	795	1 558	27 611	29 074	56 685
1986	24 456	25 706	50 162	2 474	2 649	5 123	768	798	1 567	27 698	29 153	56 852
1987	24 546	25 775	50 321	2 470	2 643	5 113	773	802	1 575	27 789	29 220	57 009
1988	24 641	25 846	50 487	2 461	2 632	5 093	774	804	1 578	27 876	29 282	57 158
1989	24 750	25 928	50 678	2 463	2 634	5 097	777	806	1 583	27 989	29 368	57 358
1990	24 872	25 998	50 869	2 466	2 636	5 102	780	809	1 589	28 118	29 443	57 561
1991	24 995	26 104	51 100	2 470	2 637	5 107	778	820	1 601	28 246	29 562	57 808
1992	25 099	26 178	51 277	2 473	2 638	5 111	791	828	1 618	28 362	29 645	58 006
1993	25 198	26 241	51 439	2 479	2 642	5 120	797	835	1 632	28 474	29 718	58 191
1994	25 304	26 317	51 621	2 486	2 646	5 132	802	840	1 642	28 592	29 803	58 395

1 Figures may not add due to rounding.

Sources: Office for National Statistics; General Register Office (Northern Ireland); General Register Office (Scotland)

From: Monthly Digest of Statistics, May 1996, Table 2.1

2.2

United Kingdom					Thousands
	Population at start of period	Average annual change			Overall annual change
		Live births	Deaths	Net natural change	Other [1]	
Census enumerated						
1901-1911	38,237	1,091	624	467	-82	385
1911-1921	42,082	975	689	286	-92	194
1921-1931	44,027	824	555	268	-67	201
1931-1951	46,038	785	598	188	25	213
Mid-year estimates						
1951-1961	50,287	839	593	246	6	252
1961-1971	52,807	963	639	324	-12	312
1971-1981	55,928	736	666	69	-27	42
1981-1991	56,352	757	655	103	43	146
1991-1994	57,808	773	642	132	64	196
Mid-year projections[2]						
1994-2001	58,395	724	639	85	68	154
2001-2011	59,472	679	626	54	49	102
2011-2021	60,493	678	629	50	14	64
2021-2031	61,130	644	685	-41	0	-41

1 Includes net civilian migration and other adjustments.
2 1994-based projections.

Source: Office for National Statistics; Government Actuary's Department; General Register Office (Scotland); General Register Office (Northern Ireland)

From: Social Trends 1996, Table 1.2

2.3 Population: by age and gender

United Kingdom						Percentages
	Under 16	16-39	40-64	65-79	80 and over	All ages (=100%) (millions)
Mid-year estimates						
1961	25	31	32	10	2	52.8
1971	25	31	30	11	2	55.9
1981	22	35	28	12	3	56.4
1991	20	35	29	12	4	57.8
1994	21	35	29	12	4	58.4
Males	22	36	29	11	2	28.6
Females	20	33	29	13	5	29.8
Mid-year projections[1]						
2001	20	33	31	11	4	59.5
2011	18	30	35	12	4	60.5
2021	18	30	34	14	5	61.1
2031	17	28	32	17	6	60.7
Males	18	29	32	16	5	30.1
Females	17	27	31	18	8	30.6

1 1994-based projections.

Source: Office for National Statistics; Government Actuary's Department; General Register Office (Scotland); General Register Office (Northern Ireland)

From: Social Trends 1996, Table 1.5

2.4 Population: by ethnic group and age, Spring 1995

Great Britain   Percentages

	Under 16	16-29	30-44	45-59	60 and over	All ages (=100%) (thousands)
Ethnic minority group						
Black[1]	29.0	25.5	27.0	11.3	7.2	869
Indian	25.3	26.0	25.5	16.0	7.2	844
Pakistani/Bangladeshi	40.6	26.4	19.4	9.3	4.3	725
Other[2]	37.2	23.3	26.0	9.6	3.9	773
All ethnic minority groups	32.6	25.3	24.6	11.7	5.8	3,211
White	20.1	19.0	21.6	18.3	20.9	52,844
All ethnic groups[3]	20.9	19.4	21.8	18.0	20.1	56,072

1 Includes Caribbean, African and other Black people of non-mixed origin.
2 Includes Chinese, other ethnic minority groups of non-mixed origin and those of mixed origin.
3 Includes ethnic group not stated.
Source: Labour Force Survey, Office for National Statistics

From: Social Trends 1996, Table 1.7

2.5 Conceptions: by marital status and outcome

England & Wales   Percentages

	1971	1981	1991	1992	1993
Inside marriage					
Maternities	72.6	65.9	51.9	51.2	51.2
Legal abortions[1]	5.2	5.6	4.4	4.4	4.3
Outside marriage					
Maternities inside marriage	8.1	5.5	3.7	3.6	3.5
Maternities outside marriage[2]					
Joint registration	3.5	6.8	18.9	19.9	20.2
Sole registration	4.1	4.8	6.0	5.9	6.0
Legal abortions[1]	6.7	11.4	15.0	14.9	14.9
All conceptions (=100%)(thousands)	835	752	854	828	819

1 Legal terminations under the 1967 Abortion Act.
2 Births outside marriage can be registered by the mother only (sole registration) or by both parents (joint registration).
Source: Office for National Statistics

From: Social Trends 1996, Table 2.26

2.6 Births

United Kingdom   Annual averages or calendar years (Thousands)

| | Live births | | | | Rates | | | | |
	Total	Male	Female	Sex ratio	Crude birth rate[1]	General fertility rate[2]	TPFR[3]	Still-births[4]	Still-birth rate[4]
1900 - 02	1 095	558	537	1 037	28.6	115.1	..	..	..
1910 - 12	1 037	528	508	1 039	24.6	99.4	..	..	..
1920 - 22	1 018	522	496	1 052	23.1	93.0	..	..	..
1930 - 32	750	383	367	1 046	16.3	66.5	..	..	..
1940 - 42	723	372	351	1 062	15.0	..	1.89	26	..
1950 - 52	803	413	390	1 061	16.0	73.7	2.21	18	..
1960 - 62	946	487	459	1 063	17.9	90.3	2.80	18	..
1970 - 72	880	453	427	1 064	15 8	82.5	2.36	12	13
1980 - 82	735	377	358	1 053	13.0	62.5	1.83	5	7
1980	754	386	368	1 050	13.4	64.9	1.89	6	7
1981	731	375	356	1 053	13.0	62.1	1.81	5	7
1982	719	369	350	1 054	12.8	60.6	1.78	5	6
1983	721	371	351	1 058	12.8	60.2	1.77	4	6
1984	730	373	356	1 049	12.9	60.3	1.77	4	6
1985	751	385	366	1 053	13.3	61.4	1.80	4	6
1986	755	387	368	1 053	13.3	61.1	1.78	4	5
1987	776	398	378	1 053	13.6	62.3	1.82	4	5
1988	788	403	384	1 049	13.8	63.2	1.84	4	5
1989	777	398	379	1 051	13.6	62.4	1.81	4	5
1990	799	409	390	1 049	13.9	64.2	1.84	4	5
1991	793	406	386	1 052	13.7	63.6	1.82	4	5
1992	781	400	380	1 052	13.5	63.4	1.80	3	4
1993	762	391	371	1 054	13.1	62.4	1.76	4	6
1994	751	385	365	1 054	129.0	61.5	1.74	4	6

1 Rate per 1 000 population.
2 Rate per 1 000 women aged 15 - 44.
3 Total period fertility rate is the average number of children which would be born per woman if women experienced the age-specific fertility rates of the period in question throughout their child-bearing life span. UK figures for the years 1970-72 and earlier are estimates.
4 Figures given are based on stillbirths of 28 completed weeks gestation or more. On 1 October 1992 the legal definition of a stillbirth was altered to include babies born dead between 24 and 27 completed weeks gestation. Between 1 October and 31 December 1992 there were 258 babies born dead between 24 and 27 completed weeks gestation (216 in England and Wales, 35 in Scotland and 7 in Northern Ireland). If these babies were included in the stillbirth figures given, the stillbirth rate would be 5 for the UK and England and Wales while the Scotland and Northern Ireland stillbirth rate would remain as stated.

Source: Office for National Statistics; General Register Office (Scotland); General Register Office (Northern Ireland)   *From: Annual Abstract of Statistics 1996, Table 2.13*

2.7 Births and deaths

United Kingdom

Millions

1 1992-based projections.
2 Includes deaths of non-civilians and merchant seamen who died outside the country.

Source: Office for National Statistics; Government Actuary's Department; General Register Office (Scotland); General Register Office (Northern Ireland)

From: Social Trends 1996, Chart 1.12

2.8 Deaths: by gender and age

United Kingdom — Rates

	Death rates per 1,000 in each age group							All deaths (thou-sands)
	Under 1[1]	1-15	16-39	40-64	65-79	80 and over	All ages	
Males								
1961	26.3	0.6	1.3	11.7	65.7	193.5	12.6	322.0
1971	20.2	0.5	1.1	11.4	59.9	174.0	12.1	328.5
1981	12.7	0.4	1.0	10.1	56.1	167.5	12.0	329.1
1991	8.3	0.3	1.0	7.3	48.2	148.2	11.1	314.4
1994	6.9	0.2	0.9	6.6	44.7	141.4	10.6	302.1
Females								
1961	18.2	0.7	0.8	6.5	41.0	156.8	11.4	309.8
1971	15.5	0.4	0.6	6.3	35.3	138.0	11.0	316.5
1981	9.6	0.3	0.5	5.8	32.1	126.2	11.4	328.8
1991	6.3	0.2	0.5	4.5	29.1	112.2	11.2	331.8
1994	5.4	0.2	0.5	4.1	27.5	108.6	10.9	323.8

1 Rate per 1,000 live births.

Source: Office for National Statistics; General Register Office (Scotland); General Register Office (Northern Ireland)

From: Social Trends 1996, Table 1.14

2.9 Marriages

United Kingdom — Numbers

	1983	1984	1985	1986	1987	1988	1989	1990	1991	1992	1993
Marriages	389 286	395 797	393 117	393 939	397 937	394 049	392 042	375 410	349 739	356 013	341 246
Persons marrying per 1 000 resident population	*13.8*	*14.0*	*13.9*	*13.9*	*14.0*	*13.8*	*13.7*	*13.1*	*12.1*	*12.3*	*11.7*
Previous marital status											
Bachelors	288 713	293 645	291 171	290 144	296 290	289 493	288 478	276 512	256 538	258 567	245 623
Divorced men	86 484	88 691	88 981	91 006	89 814	92 755	92 033	88 199	83 069	87 419	85 839
Widowers	14 089	13 461	12 965	12 789	11 833	11 801	11 531	10 699	10 132	10 027	9 784
Spinsters	293 554	299 256	296 797	294 564	301 073	293 551	291 516	279 442	259 084	260 252	247 751
Divorced women	82 314	83 477	83 921	87 080	85 238	89 066	89 234	85 608	81 224	86 361	84 249
Widows	13 418	13 064	12 399	12 295	11 626	11 612	11 294	10 360	9 431	9 400	9 246
First marriage for both partners	254 620	258 997	256 594	254 237	260 459	253 150	251 572	240 729	222 369	222 142	210 236
First marriage for one partner	73 027	74 913	74 780	76 254	76 445	76 744	76 850	74 496	70 884	74 535	72 902
Remarriage for both partners	61 639	61 890	61 743	63 458	61 033	64 155	63 620	60 185	56 486	59 336	58 108
Males											
Under 21 years	37 141	33 447	30 243	25 828	24 269	20 608	19 070	15 930	13 271	11 031	8 678
21-24	127 149	127 351	123 242	119 464	118 355	109 482	102 977	92 270	79 877	74 458	64 944
25-29	99 855	105 799	109 896	114 007	119 808	120 939	123 491	122 800	115 637	118 255	114 014
30-34	45 794	47 325	47 594	49 287	51 389	53 865	56 442	56 966	56 970	62 470	63 809
35-44	43 538	45 955	46 265	48 583	48 598	51 329	51 411	49 984	48 147	51 125	50 598
45-54	18 990	19 358	19 652	20 376	19 788	21 544	22 329	21 996	20 915	23 290	23 825
55 and over	16 819	16 562	16 225	16 394	15 730	16 282	16 322	15 464	14 922	15 384	15 378
Females											
Under 21 years	96 859	90 301	82 209	72 466	68 629	59 284	54 256	45 626	38 305	32 618	26 624
21-24	132 020	136 244	137 437	138 219	140 509	134 122	128 411	119 037	105 505	102 494	92 919
25-29	70 284	76 566	80 105	85 316	90 911	95 338	100 531	103 209	99 851	105 223	104 469
30-34	32 163	32 998	33 424	35 237	36 643	39 680	41 989	42 794	43 617	48 514	49 656
35-44	33 156	34 854	35 380	37 515	36 978	39 534	40 290	38 983	37 582	40 075	40 081
45-54	14 325	14 716	14 892	15 414	15 001	16 570	17 172	16 825	16 473	18 504	18 798
55 and over	10 479	10 118	9 670	9 772	9 260	9 521	9 393	8 936	8 406	8 585	8 699

Source: Office for National Statistics

From: Annual Abstract of Statistics 1996, Table 2.10

2.10 Divorce: by duration of marriage

United Kingdom					Percentages
	1961	1971	1981	1991	1993
0-2 years	1	1	2	9	8
3-4 years	10	12	19	14	14
5-9 years	31	31	29	27	28
10-14 years	23	19	20	18	18
15-19 years	} 14	{ 13	13	13	12
20-24 years		{ 10	9	10	10
25-29 years	} 21	{ 6	5	5	5
30 years and over		{ 9	5	4	4
All durations (=100%) (thousands)	27.0	79.2	155.6	171.1	180.0

Source: Office for National Statistics; General Register Office (Scotland); General Register Office (Northern Ireland)

From: Social Trends 1996, Table 2.20

2.11 Divorces granted: by ground, 1993

England, Wales & Northern Ireland

Percentages

Source: Office for National Statistics; General Register Office (Northern Ireland)

From: Social Trends 1996, Chart 2.21

three

Employment

Definitions and sources

The labour force in employment - a count, obtained from household surveys and censuses, of employees, self-employed persons, participants in government employment and training programmes, and persons doing unpaid family work.

The ILO unemployed - an International Labour Organisation (ILO) recommended measure, used in household surveys such as the Labour Force Survey, which counts as unemployed those aged 16 and over who are without a job, are available to start work in the next two weeks, who have been seeking a job in the last four weeks or are waiting to start a job already obtained.

ILO unemployment rate - the percentage of the **economically active** who are **ILO unemployed.**

The economically active - the **labour force in employment** plus the **ILO unemployed.**

The economically inactive - people who are neither part of the labour force in employment nor ILO unemployed. For example, all people under 16, those looking after a home or retired, or those permanently unable to work.

The population of working age - males aged 16 to 64 years and females aged 16 to 59 years.

Economic activity rate - the percentage of the population in a given age group which is in the labour force.

For other sources see: *Guide to Official Statistics, 1996 edition* (520 pages approximately, fully indexed) HMSO.

Labour Market Trends, HMSO.

3.1 Labour force: by age

Great Britain — Thousands

	16-24	25-44	45-59	60-64	65 and over	All aged 16 and over
Estimates						
1984	6,214	12,201	7,077	1,252	429	27,172
1986	6,326	12,788	6,968	1,083	402	27,566
1991	5,684	14,256	7,311	1,102	462	28,815
1992	5,224	14,192	7,596	1,069	501	28,582
1993	4,941	14,258	7,742	1,070	443	28,454
1994	4,710	14,301	7,922	1,051	437	28,421
Projections						
1996	4,404	14,609	8,227	1,049	429	28,717
2001	4,313	14,893	8,748	1,105	409	29,469
2006	4,519	14,609	9,252	1,295	416	30,092

Source: Labour Force Survey, Office for National Statistics

From: Social Trends 1996, Table 4.2

3.2 Labour Force Survey: economic activity[1]

Great Britain Thousands, seasonally adjusted

	In employment[2]					ILO unemploy-ed	Total econom-ically active	Economic-ally inactive	All aged 16 and over
	Employees	Self-employed	On government employment and training programmes[3]	Unpaid family workers[4]	All[5]				
ALL									
Summer 1992	21 473	3 147	351	175	25 146	2 778	27 923	16 253	44 176
Autumn 1992	21 441	3 088	343	176	25 048	2 859	27 907	16 283	44 190
Winter 1992	21 385	3 084	326	152	24 947	2 957	27 905	16 299	44 203
Spring 1993	21 382	3 101	333	145	24 960	2 903	27 863	16 353	44 217
Summer 1993	21 360	3 113	329	151	24 953	2 876	27 828	16 402	44 230
Autumn 1993	21 402	3 143	323	140	25 009	2 855	27 864	16 382	44 246
Winter 1993	21 425	3 193	324	135	25 077	2 786	27 863	16 399	44 262
Spring 1994	21 486	3 208	315	140	25 149	2 712	27 861	16 417	44 277
Summer 1994	21 545	3 224	298	138	25 206	2 669	27 875	16 419	44 293
Autumn 1994	21 593	3 269	290	142	25 294	2 532	27 826	16 496	44 322
Winter 1994	21 675	3 289	278	128	25 371	2 435	27 806	16 545	44 352
Spring 1995	21 748	3 260	265	133	25 407	2 432	27 839	16 542	44 381
Summer 1995	21 874	3 249	257	125	25 505	2 416	27 921	16 489	44 410
Autumn 1995	21 939	3 247	245	131	25 562	2 396	27 959	16 489	44 447
Winter 1995	22 106	3 219	237	118	25 680	2 302	27 982	16 503	44 485
Estimated changes									
Autumn 1995 - Winter 1995	167	-27	-9	-13	118	-94	23	14	37
Per cent	0.8	-0.8	-3.5	-9.8	0.5	-3.9	0.1	0.1	0.1
MALE									
Summer 1992	11 302	2 367	231	54	13 953	1 851	15 804	5 578	21 382
Autumn 1992	11 244	2 320	221	55	13 841	1 919	15 760	5 635	21 395
Winter 1992	11 186	2 330	206	46	13 768	1 981	15 750	5 658	21 407
Spring 1993	11 168	2 316	219	41	13 744	1 948	15 692	5 728	21 420
Summer 1993	11 146	2 331	219	47	13 742	1 904	15 647	5 786	21 432
Autumn 1993	11 173	2 349	215	42	13 779	1 885	15 663	5 785	21 448
Winter 1993	11 199	2 384	217	37	13 837	1 831	15 667	5 796	21 464
Spring 1994	11 223	2 406	207	47	13 883	1 790	15 673	5 806	21 479
Summer 1994	11 246	2 427	195	49	13 916	1 775	15 691	5 804	21 495
Autumn 1994	11 306	2 462	191	44	14 004	1 670	15 673	5 843	21 516
Winter 1994	11 333	2 480	186	41	14 039	1 597	15 636	5 901	21 537
Spring 1995	11 393	2 470	173	40	14 076	1 577	15 653	5 906	21 559
Summer 1995	11 436	2 450	163	44	14 092	1 572	15 665	5 915	21 580
Autumn 1995	11 462	2 454	157	42	14 115	1 552	15 667	5 937	21 604
Winter 1995	11 547	2 421	147	35	14 150	1 515	15 665	5 964	21 629
Estimated changes									
Autumn 1995 - Winter 1995	85	-33	-10	-7	35	-37	-2	27	25
Per cent	0.7	-1.3	-6.4	-16.9	0.2	-2.4	0.0	0.5	0.1
FEMALE									
Summer 1992	10 171	780	120	121	11 192	927	12 119	10 675	22 794
Autumn 1992	10 197	768	121	121	11 207	939	12 147	10 648	22 795
Winter 1992	10 199	754	120	105	11 179	976	12 155	10 641	22 796
Spring 1993	10 214	784	114	104	11 216	955	12 171	10 625	22 797
Summer 1993	10 214	782	110	104	11 210	972	12 182	10 616	22 798
Autumn 1993	10 229	795	108	98	11 230	971	12 201	10 597	22 798
Winter 1993	10 226	809	107	98	11 240	955	12 196	10 602	22 798
Spring 1994	10 263	802	108	93	11 266	921	12 187	10 611	22 798
Summer 1994	10 300	798	103	89	11 290	894	12 184	10 614	22 798
Autumn 1994	10 286	807	99	98	11 291	862	12 153	10 653	22 806
Winter 1994	10 342	809	93	88	11 332	838	12 170	10 644	22 814
Spring 1995	10 355	791	92	93	11 331	856	12 187	10 636	22 822
Summer 1995	10 438	800	94	81	11 413	844	12 257	10 574	22 830
Autumn 1995	10 478	793	89	88	11 447	844	12 291	10 552	22 843
Winter 1995	10 559	798	90	83	11 530	787	12 317	10 539	22 856
Estimated changes									
Autumn 1995 - Winter 1995	82	5	1	-6	83	-57	26	-13	13
Per cent	0.8	0.7	1.7	-6.4	0.7	-6.8	0.2	-0.1	0.1

1 Since 1984 the definitions used in the Labour Force Survey (LFS) have been fully in line with international recommendations. For details see 'The quarterly Labour Force Survey; a new dimension to labour market statistics', *Employment Gazette*, October 1992, pp 483-490.
2 People in full-time education who also did some paid work in the reference week have been classified as in employment since Spring 1983.
3 Those on employment and training programmes have been classified as in employment since Spring 1983.
4 Unpaid family workers have been classified as in employment since Spring 1992.
5 Includes those who did not state whether they were employees or self-employed.

Source: Office for National Statistics *From: Economic Trends, May 1996, Table 4.4*

3.3 Economic activity status of mothers[1]: by age of youngest child, Spring 1994

United Kingdom   Percentages

	Lone mothers	Married[2] mothers	All mothers[1]
0-4 years			
Working full time	9	18	16
Working part time	14	33	29
Unemployed[3]	8	5	6
Inactive	69	44	49
5-10 years			
Working full time	16	21	20
Working part time	28	49	44
Unemployed[3]	10	5	6
Inactive	46	25	30
11-15 years			
Working full time	32	34	34
Working part time	29	42	40
Unemployed[3]	9	3	4
Inactive	30	20	22

1 Aged 16 to 59.
2 Includes those cohabiting.
3 Based on the ILO definition.

Source: Office for National Statistics

From: Social Focus on Women, Table 2.12

3.4 Women in employment[1]: by occupation, Spring 1994

United Kingdom

Percentages

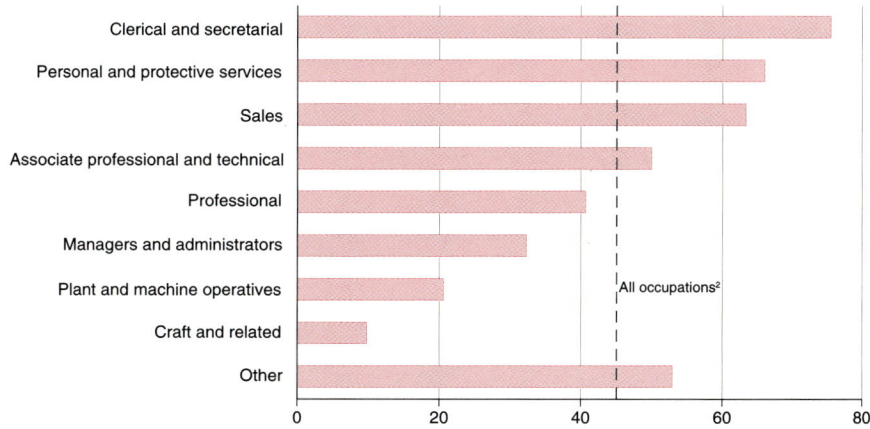

1 Percentage of those in employment in each occupation who are women.
2 Includes women who did not state their occupation.

Source: Office for National Statistics

From: Social Focus on Women, Chart 2.20

3.5 ILO unemployment rates

Percentages

	Spring quarter of each year									
	1986	1987	1988	1989	1990	1991	1992	1993	1994	1995
United Kingdom	11.2	10.8	8.8	7.2	6.8	8.4	9.7	10.3	9.6	8.6
North	14.7	13.4	13.5	11.1	10.4	11.0	11.3	11.3	11.8	10.8
Yorkshire & Humberside	12.4	11.7	11.0	8.7	7.7	8.3	10.1	10.0	9.9	8.7
East Midlands	10.2	10.3	7.7	6.8	6.6	7.3	8.8	9.1	8.3	7.5
East Anglia	8.6	8.5	5.5	4.1	4.8	6.3	7.1	8.4	7.4	7.1
South East	8.5	7.9	6.1	5.0	5.2	7.3	9.5	10.4	9.7	8.6
Greater London	10.5	9.4	8.0	6.8	6.8	9.1	12.0	13.2	13.1	11.5
Rest of South East	7.3	6.9	4.8	3.8	4.2	6.1	7.9	8.5	7.6	6.8
South West	8.9	8.6	6.2	5.2	5.0	7.6	9.1	9.2	7.5	7.8
West Midlands	12.6	12.8	8.9	7.5	6.8	9.5	10.7	11.8	10.0	9.0
North West	14.0	12.8	11.5	9.5	8.0	9.7	10.2	11.1	10.4	9.1
England	10.6	10.1	8.1	6.7	6.4	8.1	9.7	10.3	9.5	8.6
Wales	14.3	13.3	11.4	9.1	8.0	9.1	8.9	9.6	9.3	8.8
Scotland	13.9	14.9	12.0	9.7	9.3	9.3	9.5	10.2	10.0	8.3
Northern Ireland	15.8	15.2	13.9	12.6	11.6	12.2	12.3	12.5	11.7	11.0

Source: Labour Force Survey, Office for National Statistics; Department of Economic Development, Northern Ireland

From: Regional Trends 1996, Table 5.19

3.6 Unemployment rates[1]: by gender and age

United Kingdom

Percentages

	1991	1992	1993	1994	1995
Males					
16-19	16.5	18.6	22.0	20.9	19.6
20-29	12.3	15.5	16.5	14.9	14.0
30-39	7.8	10.5	10.3	10.2	8.3
40-49	5.8	7.7	8.8	7.6	7.1
50-64	8.4	10.4	11.9	11.0	9.2
65 and over	5.9	4.9	4.6	3.7	2.7
All males aged 16 and over	9.2	11.5	12.4	11.4	10.1
Females					
16-19	13.2	13.8	15.9	16.0	14.8
20-29	9.4	9.4	10.3	9.3	9.2
30-39	6.9	7.5	7.3	7.3	6.5
40-49	4.9	5.1	4.9	4.9	5.0
50-59	5.1	4.5	5.4	5.3	4.2
60 and over	4.4	4.7	4.1	3.0	2.4
All females aged 16 and over	7.2	7.3	7.6	7.3	6.8

1 Unemployment based on the ILO definition as a percentage of all economically active. At Spring each year.

Source: Labour Force Survey, Office for National Statistics

From: Social Trends 1996, Table 4.23

3.7 Labour force economic activity rates[1]: by gender and age

United Kingdom   Percentages

	16-24	25-44	45-59	60-64	65 and over	All aged 16 and over
Males						
Estimates						
1984	81.8	96.1	90.0	57.5	8.7	75.9
1986	82.6	95.9	88.8	53.8	7.9	75.2
1991	81.2	95.7	88.1	54.2	8.6	74.9
1992	77.5	95.1	87.5	52.8	8.9	73.9
1993	76.1	94.5	86.3	52.2	7.4	72.9
1994	75.1	94.1	86.1	51.0	7.6	72.6
Projections						
1996	72.4	94.2	86.4	50.4	7.5	72.2
2001	70.3	94.4	85.3	49.7	7.0	71.5
2006	69.3	94.2	83.7	49.1	6.8	70.0
Females						
Estimates						
1984	69.1	65.6	63.3	21.8	3.1	49.2
1986	70.6	67.4	64.0	19.1	2.7	50.0
1991	71.3	73.0	66.9	23.9	3.1	53.1
1992	67.5	72.8	68.4	23.4	3.6	52.8
1993	66.0	73.6	68.5	24.7	3.5	53.0
1994	64.6	73.5	69.3	25.3	3.2	53.0
Projections						
1996	63.6	74.8	70.4	26.6	3.0	53.7
2001	63.3	77.8	71.9	29.0	2.8	55.5
2006	63.2	81.3	72.6	31.9	2.9	56.7

1 The percentage of the population that is in the labour force.

Source: Labour Force Survey, Office for National Statistics

From: Social Trends 1996, Table 4.4

3.8 Temporary[1] employees: by gender and reason for taking temporary job[2], Spring 1995

United Kingdom   Percentages

	Males	Females	All
Could not find a permanent job	51.5	37.8	44.2
Did not want a permanent job	19.2	34.5	27.4
Had a contract which included a period of training	7.3	4.3	5.7
Other reasons	21.9	23.3	22.6
All persons in temporary jobs (=100%)(thousands)	720	827	1,547

1 Temporary employees are those who assess themselves to have either a seasonal, temporary or casual job or a job done under contract or for a fixed period.

2 As a main job.

Source: Labour Force Survey, Office for National Statistics

From: Social Trends 1996, Table 4.11

3.9 Proportion of employees receiving job-related training[1]: by gender and age

United Kingdom   Percentages

	1986	1991	1992	1993	1994	1995
Males						
16-29	18.1	20.3	19.5	19.2	19.5	18.1
30-64	8.0	11.8	11.9	12.0	12.8	11.6
All males aged 16 to 64	11.4	14.7	14.3	14.3	14.9	13.6
Females						
16-29	14.6	17.9	18.2	18.6	21.1	18.0
30-64	7.2	13.3	13.1	13.4	14.1	13.6
All females aged 16 to 64	9.9	14.9	14.9	15.1	16.3	15.0

1 At Spring each year.

Source: Labour Force Survey; Department for Education and Employment

From: Social Trends 1996, Table 4.29

3.10 Redundancy rates[1]: by occupation

Great Britain   Rates per 1,000 employees

	1992	1993	1994	1995
Managers and administrators	12.2	8.3	9.8	10.2
Professional	6.3	6.1	4.5	5.3
Associate professional and technical	10.6	8.5	5.7	8.1
Clerical and secretarial	14.7	9.9	7.8	10.6
Craft and related	27.9	20.7	18.2	15.7
Personal and protective services	6.9	6.9	5.8	6.3
Sales	14.8	15.5	10.0	12.6
Plant and machine operatives	22.8	22.7	16.1	12.8
Other	16.4	14.6	9.2	10.4
All occupations	15.1	12.3	9.6	10.2

1 At Spring each year.

Source: Labour Force Survey, Office for National Statistics

From: Social Trends 1996, Table 4.26

four

National accounts

Definitions and sources

National accounts provide a comprehensive and detailed framework for describing and analysing the economy as a whole and showing how various economic activities are related. They provide the basic background for decision-taking and forecasting in both Government and business. The accounts are published annually in *United Kingdom and National Accounts: the ONS 'Blue Book'* and quarterly in *UK Economic Accounts*. A definitive detailed description of the various statistical series which comprise the national accounts is given in *United Kingdom National Accounts: Sources and Methods*. In general, the United Kingdom national accounts follow the principles recommended internationally.

Gross domestic product (GDP) is a concept of the value of goods and services produced on the economic territory irrespective of to whom the benefits accrue (United Kingdom residents or non-residents). The national product indicates the activities of UK residents only on both the UK economic territory and abroad.

The level of GDP is derived from the levels of the two broadly independent analyses of GDP based on expenditure and income. Account is taken also of the changes in volume of value added derived from the output analysis of GDP, which is compiled only in index number format.

The expenditure analysis differentiates between consumption expenditure (goods and services consumed within a short time of purchase) and investment expenditure which adds to the domestic stock of physical assets (capital formation) or to those claims on non-residents which arise from the difference between exports and imports of goods and services. Estimates are compiled in both current and constant prices. The deflator implied by these current and constant price estimates at factor cost conceptually measures the price of domestic value added and is known as the 'index of total home costs'.

The income analysis identifies the different types of factor incomes derived from domestic production such as income from employment, from self-employment, profits and rent. It is compiled only in current price terms but a constant price equivalent is derived by deflating total incomes by the total home costs deflator.

The output analysis provides estimates of the contribution of each industry. The production and construction industries account for about two-fifths of total output. Agriculture and the services industries, for example, distribution, transport, and financial services, make up the remainder. Estimates are available only at constant prices in index number form. The *Monthly Digest of Statistics* contains monthly detail for production industries.

Gross national disposable income at market prices is a concept of the United Kingdom's command over resources. It is based on GDP at market prices, adjusted for the effect of changes in the terms of trade, for net property income from abroad and net current transfers abroad.

For other sources see: *Guide to Official Statistics, 1996 edition* (520 pages approximately, fully indexed) HMSO.

4.1 Gross national and domestic product[1]

£ million

| | At current prices | | | | | | At 1990 prices | | |
| | At market prices | | | | At factor cost | | | | |
	Gross domestic product "Money GDP"	Net property income from abroad	Gross national product	less Factor cost adjust-ment[2]	Gross domestic product[3]	Gross national product[4]	Gross domestic product at market prices	less Factor cost adjust-ment[5]	Gross domestic product at factor cost
1988	471 430	4 566	475 996	70 002	401 428	405 994	537 215	71 469	465 746
1989	515 957	3 502	519 459	74 198	441,759	445 261	548 940	72 712	476 228
1990	551 118	1 269	552 387	72 232	478 886	480 155	551 118	72 232	478 886
1991	575 674	150	575 824	79 421	496 253	496 403	540 308	71 395	468 913
1992	598 916	3 124	602 040	80 784	518 132	521 256	537 448	70 992	466 456
1993	631 158	2 197	633 355	83 133	548 025	550 222	548 947	71 822	477 125
1994	668 255	8 691	676 946	89 078	579 177	587 868	570 290	73 913	496 377
1995	700 890	9 572	710 462	96 631	604 259	613 831	584 340	75 533	508 807
Seasonally adjusted									
1992 Q1	146 497	976	147 473	20 547	125 950	126 926	133 943	17 943	116 037
Q2	149 908	693	150 601	20 136	129 772	130 465	134 056	17 806	116 250
Q3	151 003	791	151 794	20 111	130 892	131 683	134 696	17 817	116 879
Q4	151 508	664	152 172	19 990	131 518	132 182	134 753	17 463	117 290
1993 Q1	154 499	423	154 922	20 848	133 651	134 074	136 067	18 004	118 063
Q2	156 353	714	157 067	20 379	135 974	136 688	136 421	17 792	118 629
Q3	159 746	580	160 326	20 820	138 926	139 506	137 783	17 992	119 791
Q4	160 560	480	161 040	21 086	139 474	139 954	138 676	18 034	120 642
1994 Q1	163 441	2 528	165 969	21 517	141 924	144 452	140 301	18 199	122 102
Q2	165 760	2 231	167 991	22 064	143 696	145 927	142 029	18 371	123 658
Q3	168 773	2 071	170 844	22 468	146 305	148 376	143 425	18 580	124 845
Q4	170 281	1 861	172 142	23 029	147 252	149 113	144 535	18 763	125 772
1995 Q1	172 513	1 754	174 267	23 720	148 793	150 547	145 079	18 811	126 268
Q2	174 659	2 512	177 171	23 930	150 729	153 241	145 693	18 882	126 811
Q3	175 933	2 571	178 504	24 269	151 664	154 235	146 503	18 900	127 603
Q4	177 785	2 735	180 520	24 712	153 073	155 808	147 065	18 940	128 125
1996 Q1	179 567	2 908	182 475	24 994	154 573	157 481	147 605	18 979	128 626
Percentage change, latest year on previous year									
1995	4.9		5.0	8.5	4.3	4.4	2.5	2.2	2.5
Percentage change, latest quarter on previous quarter									
1996 Q1	1.0		1.1	1.1	1.0	1.1	0.4	0.2	0.4
Percentage change, latest quarter on corresponding quarter of previous year									
1996 Q1	4.1		4.7	5.4	3.9	4.6	1.7	0.9	1.9

1 Estimates are given to the nearest £ million and in case of indices to one decimal place but cannot be regarded as accurate to this degree. Estimates at current market prices are affected by the abolition of domestic rates and the introduction of the community charge.

2 *Equals* taxes on expenditure *less* subsidies.

3 The factor cost estimate of GDP is obtained from the market price estimates by subtracting the factor cost adjustment.

4 Gross national product *equals* Gross domestic product *plus* Net property income from abroad.

5 *Represents* Taxes on expenditure *less* Subsidies both valued at 1990 prices.

Source: Office for National Statistics

From: UK Economic Accounts 1996 Q1, Table A1

4.2 Gross national and domestic product[1]

1990 = 100

	Value indices at current prices		Volume indices at 1990 prices			Implied gross domestic product deflator[4]	
	Gross domestic product at market prices[2]	Gross domestic product at factor cost	Gross national disposable income at market prices[3]	Gross domestic product at market prices	Gross domestic product at factor cost	At market prices	At factor cost[5]
1988	85.5	83.8	97.8	97.5	97.3	87.8	86.2
1989	93.6	92.2	99.8	99.6	99.4	94.0	92.8
1990	100.0	100.0	100.0	100.0	100.0	100.0	100.0
1991	104.5	103.6	98.8	98.0	97.9	106.5	105.8
1992	108.7	108.2	98.5	97.5	97.4	111.4	111.1
1993	114.5	114.4	100.6	99.6	99.6	115.0	114.9
1994	121.3	120.9	105.1	103.5	103.7	117.2	116.7
1995	127.2	126.2	106.7	106.0	106.2	119.9	118.8
1992 Q1	106.3	105.2	98.2	97.2	96.9	109.4	108.5
Q2	108.8	108.4	98.5	97.3	97.1	111.8	111.6
Q3	109.6	109.3	99.0	97.8	97.6	112.1	112.0
Q4	110.0	109.9	98.5	97.8	98.0	112.4	112.1
1993 Q1	112.1	111.6	99.5	98.8	98.6	113.5	113.2
Q2	113.5	113.6	100.0	99.0	99.1	114.6	114.6
Q3	115.9	116.0	101.2	100.0	100.1	115.9	116.0
Q4	116.5	116.5	101.9	100.7	100.8	115.8	115.6
1994 Q1	118.6	118.5	103.7	101.8	102.0	116.5	116.2
Q2	120.3	120.0	104.4	103.1	103.3	116.7	116.2
Q3	122.5	122.2	105.4	104.1	104.3	117.7	117.2
Q4	123.6	123.0	106.8	104.9	105.1	117.8	117.1
1995 Q1	125.2	124.3	106.1	105.3	105.5	118.9	117.8
Q2	126.8	125.9	106.7	105.7	105.9	119.9	118.9
Q3	127.7	126.7	106.9	106.3	106.6	120.1	118.9
Q4	129.0	127.9	107.2	106.7	107.0	120.9	119.5
1996 Q1	130.3	129.1	108.3	107.1	107.4	121.7	120.2

Percentage change, latest year on previous year

1995	4.9	4.3	1.6	2.5	2.5	2.4	1.8

Percentage change, latest quarter on previous quarter

1996 Q1	1.0	1.0	0.9	0.4	0.4	0.6	0.6

Percentage change, latest quarter on corresponding quarter of previous year

1996 Q1	4.1	3.9	2.1	1.7	1.9	2.3	2.0

1 These estimates are given to one decimal place but this does not imply that they can be regarded as accurate to the last digit shown.
2 "Money GDP"
3 Also known as Real national disposable income (RNDI).
4 Based on sum of expenditure components of GDP at current and constant prices.
5 Also known as the Index of total home costs.

Source: Office for National Statistics

From: UK Economic Accounts 1996 Q1, Table A1

4.3 Gross domestic product: by category of expenditure

£ million

	Domestic expenditure on goods and services at market prices														
	General government final consumption				Gross domestic fixed capital formation	Value of physical increase in stocks and work in progress[3]	Total	Exports of goods and services	Total final expenditure	less Imports of goods and services	Stat-ist-cal dis-crep-ancy (exp-end-iture)	Gross domestic product at market prices	less Taxes on expen-diture[4]	Sub-sidies	Gross domestic product at factor cost
	Cons-umers' expen-diture[2]	Central gover-nment	Local autho-rities	Total											
At current prices															
1988	299 449	57 522	36 119	93 641	91 530	4 333	488 953	107 273	596 226	124 796	-	**471 430**	76 039	6 037	**401 428**
1989	327 363	63 294	38 502	101 796	105 443	2 677	537 279	121 486	658 765	142 808	-	**515 957**	79 980	5 782	**441 759**
1990	347 527	70 108	42 826	112 934	107 577	-1 800	566 238	133 165	699 403	148 285	-	**551 118**	78 298	6 066	**478 886**
1991	365 469	76 985	47 120	124 105	97 747	-4 927	582 394	134 289	716 683	141 009	-	**575 674**	85 416	5 995	**496 253**
1992	383 490	82 259	49 616	131 875	93 642	-1 937	607 070	142 114	749 184	150 268	-	**598 916**	87 521	6 737	**518 132**
1993	406 399	89 398	48 683	138 081	94 293	329	639 102	159 997	799 099	167 941	-	**631 158**	90 336	7 203	**548 025**
1994	427 276	93 601	50 513	144 114	99 217	3 732	674 339	176 065	850 404	182 149	-	**668 255**	96 138	7 060	**579 177**
1995	447 247	96 663	52 811	149 474	105 385	3 851	705 957	197 600	903 557	203 086	419	**700 890**	103 597	6 966	**604 259**
Unadjusted															
1992 Q1	89 944	20 191	12 179	32 370	25 156	-872	146 598	33 398	179 996	35 385			21 674	1 834	
Q2	93 472	20 500	12 317	32 817	21 390	-106	147 573	35 379	182 952	37 678			21 380	1 675	
Q3	98 460	20 689	12 438	33 127	23 023	278	154 888	34 901	189 789	38 048			22 110	1 566	
Q4	101 614	20 879	12 682	33 561	24 073	-1 237	158 011	38 436	196 447	39 157			22 357	1 662	
1993 Q1	95 341	21 193	12 758	33 951	25 273	-1 465	153 100	38 715	191 815	40 373			22 003	1 996	
Q2	98 134	22 515	11 813	34 328	21 484	1 137	155 083	38 742	193 825	42 128			21 882	1 744	
Q3	105 017	22 773	11 919	34 692	23 179	468	163 356	40 488	203 844	43 163			23 000	1 200	
Q4	107 907	22 917	12 193	35 110	24 357	189	167 563	42 052	209 615	42 277			23 451	2 263	
1994 Q1	100 646	23 199	12 436	35 635	26 084	-314	162 051	41 307	203 358	42 761			22 499	1 633	
Q2	103 280	23 360	12 513	35 873	22 313	2 770	164 236	43 106	207 342	45 910			23 742	1 629	
Q3	110 254	23 470	12 630	36 100	24 509	696	171 559	45 017	216 576	46 529			24 421	1 490	
Q4	113 096	23 572	12 934	36 506	26 311	580	176 493	46 635	223 128	46 949			25 476	2 308	
1995 Q1	105 937	23 777	13 203	36 980	27 198	-1 129	168 986	47 802	216 788	46 662			24 729	1 546	
Q2	108 635	24 152	13 175	37 327	24 512	2 734	173 208	48 081	221 289	51 544			25 512	1 571	
Q3	114 700	24 299	13 199	37 498	26 128	1 551	179 877	50 083	229 960	53 173			26 325	1 496	
Q4	117 975	24 435	13 234	37 669	27 547	695	183 886	51 634	235 520	51 707			27 031	2 353	
1996 Q1	111 296	24 586	13 293	37 879	28 290	-524	176 941	51 513	228 454	53 162			26 053	1 695	
Seasonally adjusted															
1992 Q1	93 716	20 191	12 263	32 454	23 520	-1 595	148 095	34 613	182 708	36 211	-	**146 497**	22 175	1 628	**125 950**
Q2	95 615	20 500	12 289	32 789	23 398	-311	151 491	35 567	187 058	37 150	-	**149 908**	21 819	1 683	**129 772**
Q3	96 528	20 689	12 477	33 166	23 357	167	153 112	35 011	188 123	37 120	-	**151 003**	21 823	1 712	**130 892**
Q4	97 631	20 879	12 587	33 466	23 473	-198	154 372	36 923	191 295	39 787	-	**151 508**	21 704	1 714	**131 518**
1993 Q1	99 461	21 193	12 725	33 918	23 712	-400	156 691	39 614	196 305	41 806	-	**154 499**	22 642	1 794	**133 651**
Q2	100 568	22 515	11 834	34 349	23 475	91	158 483	39 049	197 532	41 179	-	**156 353**	22 210	1 831	**135 974**
Q3	102 737	22 773	11 987	34 760	23 337	612	161 446	40 236	201 682	41 936	-	**159 746**	22 617	1 797	**138 926**
Q4	103 633	22 917	12 137	35 054	23 769	26	162 482	41 098	203 580	43 020	-	**160 560**	22 867	1 781	**139 474**
1994 Q1	104 916	23 199	12 388	35 587	24 667	277	165 447	42 089	207 536	44 095	-	**163 441**	23 270	1 753	**141 924**
Q2	106 056	23 360	12 526	35 886	24 132	1 056	167 130	43 446	210 576	44 816	-	**165 760**	23 821	1 757	**143 696**
Q3	107 584	23 470	12 692	36 162	24 732	1 057	169 535	44 671	214 206	45 433	-	**168 773**	24 250	1 782	**146 305**
Q4	108 720	23 572	12 907	36 479	25 686	1 342	172 227	45 859	218 086	47 805	-	**170 281**	24 797	1 768	**147 252**
1995 Q1	110 045	23 777	13 173	36 950	25 872	-569	172 298	48 263	220 561	48 129	81	**172 513**	25 450	1 730	**148 793**
Q2	111 465	24 152	13 183	37 335	26 528	1 048	176 376	48 386	224 762	50 204	101	**174 659**	25 646	1 716	**150 729**
Q3	112 194	24 299	13 209	37 508	26 355	1 727	177 784	50 075	227 859	52 041	115	**175 933**	26 013	1 744	**151 664**
Q4	113 543	24 435	13 246	37 681	26 630	1 645	179 499	50 876	230 375	52 712	122	**177 785**	26 488	1 776	**153 073**
1996 Q1	115 582	24 586	13 263	37 849	26 905	1 744	182 080	51 725	233 805	54 345	107	**179 567**	26 809	1 815	**154 573**
Percentage change, latest year on previous year															
1995	4.7	3.3	4.5	3.7	6.2		4.7	12.2	6.3	11.5		4.9	7.8	-1.3	4.3
Percentage change, latest quarter on previous quarter															
1996 Q1	1.8	0.6	0.1	0.4	1.0		1.4	1.7	1.5	3.1		1.0	1.2	2.2	1.0
Percentage change, latest quarter on corresponding quarter of previous year															
1996 Q1	5.0	3.4	0.7	2.4	4.0		5.7	7.2	6.0	12.9		4.1	5.3	4.9	3.9

1 Estimates are given to the nearest £ million but cannot be regarded as accurate to this degree.
2. This series is affected by the abolition of domestic rates and the introduction of the community charge.
3. Quarterly alignment adjustment included in this series.
4. Proceeds from the National Lottery paid to the Lottery Distribution Fund are included in taxes on expenditure from 1994 Q4.

Source: Office for National Statistics

From: UK Economic Accounts 1996 Q1, Table A2

4.4 Gross domestic product: by category of expenditure[1]

£ million

| | Domestic expenditure on goods and services at market prices | | | | | | | | | | | | |
| | General government final consumption | | | | | | | | | | | | |
	Consumers' expenditure[2]	Central government	Local authorities	Total	Gross domestic fixed capital formation	Value of physical increase in stocks and work in progress[2]	Total	Exports of goods and services	Total final expenditure	less Imports of goods and services	Statistical discrepancy (exp enditure)	Gross domestic product at market prices	less Taxes on expenditure[3]	Gross domestic product at factor cost
Revalued at 1990 prices														
1988	334 591	67 588	41 024	108 612	105 164	5 094	553 461	121 197	674 658	137 443	-	**537 215**	71 469	**465 746**
1989	345 406	68 836	41 303	110 139	111 470	2 704	569 719	126 836	696 555	147 615	-	**548 940**	72 712	**476 228**
1990	347 527	70 108	42 826	112 934	107 577	-1 800	566 238	133 165	699 403	148 285	-	**551 118**	72 232	**478 886**
1991	340 037	71 811	44 034	115 845	97 403	-4 631	548 654	132 252	680 906	140 598	-	**540 308**	71 395	**468 913**
1992	339 652	72 039	43 693	115 732	95 973	-1 699	549 658	137 693	687 351	149 903	-	**537 448**	70 992	**466 456**
1993	348 015	74 455	41 537	115 992	96 586	312	560 905	142 451	703 356	154 409	-	**548 947**	71 822	**477 125**
1994	356 914	75 950	42 257	118 207	99 417	2 917	577 455	155 566	733 021	162 731	-	**570 290**	73 913	**496 377**
1995	364 045	76 407	43 294	119 701	99 302	3 258	586 306	166 773	753 079	169 092	353	**584 340**	75 533	**508 807**
Unadjusted														
1992 Q1	80 765	18 310	11 016	29 326	25 384	-811	134 664	32 694	167 358	35 564			17 734	
Q2	82 371	17 957	10 870	28 827	21 801	-76	132 923	34 410	167 333	38 152			17 282	
Q3	87 191	17 865	10 857	28 722	23 671	365	139 949	33 995	173 944	38 713			17 750	
Q4	89 325	17 907	10 950	28 857	25 117	-1 177	142 122	36 594	178 716	37 474			18 226	
1993 Q1	82 763	18 007	10 988	28 995	26 226	-1 483	136 501	34 490	170 991	37 187			17 799	
Q2	83 747	18 741	10 063	28 804	21 894	1 239	135 684	34 600	170 284	38 520			17 338	
Q3	89 556	18 850	10 191	29 041	23 605	408	142 610	35 833	178 443	39 697			18 012	
Q4	91 949	18 857	10 295	29 152	24 861	148	146 110	37 528	183 638	39 005			18 673	
1994 Q1	85 012	18 946	10 549	29 495	26 783	-347	140 943	36 919	177 862	39 234			17 894	
Q2	85 917	18 986	10 453	29 439	22 372	2 234	139 962	38 081	178 043	40 599			18 101	
Q3	91 849	19 009	10 568	29 577	24 373	533	146 332	39 264	185 596	41 075			18 603	
Q4	94 136	19 009	10 687	29 696	25 889	497	150 218	41 302	191 520	41 823			19 315	
1995 Q1	86 893	18 956	10 945	29 901	26 660	-1 092	142 362	40 969	183 331	39 901			18 561	
Q2	88 202	19 129	10 729	29 858	23 060	2 331	143 451	40 333	183 784	42 695			18 680	
Q3	93 137	19 152	10 826	29 978	24 298	1 560	148 973	42 023	190 996	43 796			18 883	
Q4	95 813	19 170	10 794	29 964	25 284	459	151 520	43 448	194 968	42 700			19 409	
1996 Q1	89 105	19 182	10 794	29 976	26 055	-415	144 721	42 682	187 403	43 356			18 776	
Seasonally adjusted														
1992 Q1	84 322	18 310	11 030	29 340	24 139	-1 271	136 530	33 856	170 386	36 443	-	**133 943**	17 906	**116 037**
Q2	84 717	17 957	10 834	28 791	24 040	-404	137 144	34 611	171 755	37 699	-	**134 056**	17 806	**116 250**
Q3	85 281	17 865	10 907	28 772	23 829	231	138 113	34 246	172 359	37 663	-	**134 696**	17 817	**116 879**
Q4	85 332	17 907	10 922	28 829	23 965	-255	137 871	34 980	172 851	38 098	-	**134 753**	17 463	**117 290**
1993 Q1	86 271	18 007	10 939	28 946	24 382	-432	139 167	35 438	174 605	38 538	-	**136 067**	18 004	**118 063**
Q2	86 488	18 741	10 079	28 820	23 805	190	139 303	34 967	174 270	37 849	-	**136 421**	17 792	**118 629**
Q3	87 414	18 850	10 237	29 087	23 986	369	140 856	35 612	176 468	38 685	-	**137 783**	17 992	**119 791**
Q4	87 842	18 857	10 282	29 139	24 413	185	141 579	36 434	178 013	39 337	-	**138 676**	18 034	**120 642**
1994 Q1	88 542	18 946	10 450	29 396	25 000	168	143 106	37 659	180 765	40 464	-	**140 301**	18 199	**122 102**
Q2	88 750	18 986	10 538	29 524	24 499	694	143 467	38 536	182 003	39 974	-	**142 029**	18 371	**123 658**
Q3	89 465	19 009	10 594	29 603	24 674	697	144 439	39 066	183 505	40 080	-	**143 425**	18 580	**124 845**
Q4	90 157	19 009	10 675	29 684	25 244	1 358	146 443	40 305	186 748	42 213	-	**144 535**	18 763	**125 772**
1995 Q1	90 337	18 956	10 830	29 786	25 317	-665	144 775	41 433	186 208	41 198	69	**145 079**	18 811	**126 268**
Q2	91 036	19 129	10 807	29 936	24 916	820	146 708	40 844	187 552	41 944	85	**145 693**	18 882	**126 811**
Q3	91 044	19 152	10 819	29 971	24 518	1 590	147 123	42 131	189 254	42 848	97	**146 503**	18 900	**127 603**
Q4	91 628	19 170	10 838	30 008	24 551	1 513	147 700	42 365	190 065	43 102	102	**147 065**	18 940	**128 125**
1996 Q1	92 484	19 182	10 846	30 028	24 927	1 520	148 959	42 913	191 872	44 356	89	**147 605**	18 979	**128 626**
Percentage change, latest year on previous year														
1995	2.0	0.6	2.5	1.3	-0.1		1.5	7.2	2.7	3.9		2.5	2.2	2.5
Percentage change, latest quarter on previous quarter														
1996 Q1	0.9	0.1	0.1	0.1	1.5		0.9	1.3	1.0	2.9		0.4	0.2	0.4
Percentage change, latest quarter on corresponding quarter of previous year														
1996 Q1	2.4	1.2	0.1	0.8	-1.5		2.9	3.6	3.0	7.7		1.7	0.9	1.9

1 Estimates are given to the nearest £ million but cannot be regarded as accurate to this degree.
2 Quarterly alignment adjustment included in this series.
3 *Represents* Taxes on expenditure *less* subsides, both valued at 1990 prices.

Source: Office for National Statistics

From: UK Economic Accounts 1996 Q1, Table A2

4.5 Gross domestic product at factor cost: by category of income[1]

£ million

	Income from employment	Gross trading profits of companies [2,3,4,5]	Gross trading surplus of public corpora-tions[3,5]	Gross trading surplus of general government enterprises[3]	Other income[6]	Total domestic income[7]	*less* Stock appreciation	Statistical discrepancy (income)	Gross domestic product at factor cost
At current prices									
1988	256 537	64 377	7 554	-32	79 367	407 803	6 375	-	**401 428**
1989	284 372	67 195	6 528	199	90 526	448 820	7 061	-	**441 759**
1990	313 753	65 703	3 801	12	101 748	485 017	6 131	-	**478 886**
1991	330 767	59 455	1 809	-36	106 268	498 263	2 010	-	**496 253**
1992	342 015	61 856	2 361	206	113 472	519 910	1 778	-	**518 132**
1993	351 819	74 820	3 454	193	120 089	550 375	2 350	-	**548 025**
1994	364 946	86 468	4 230	490	127 077	583 211	4 034	-	**579 177**
1995	377 895	91 027	4 634	613	135 172	609 341	4 902	-180	**604 259**
Unadjusted									
1992 Q1	84 497	15 014	314	18	27 616	127 459	921		
Q2	85 468	14 672	694	36	28 276	129 146	476		
Q3	85 896	14 201	558	96	28 727	129 478	-111		
Q4	86 154	17 969	795	56	28 853	133 827	492		
1993 Q1	87 118	17 003	628	8	29 500	134 257	1 420		
Q2	87 637	17 574	1 004	74	29 779	136 068	397		
Q3	88 508	18 420	737	54	30 223	137 942	233		
Q4	88 556	21 823	1 085	57	30 587	142 108	300		
1994 Q1	90 149	20 424	331	212	30 999	142 115	746		
Q2	90 653	20 388	1 354	82	31 540	144 017	806		
Q3	91 815	21 314	1 177	94	32 055	146 455	923		
Q4	92 329	24 342	1 368	102	32 483	150 624	1 559		
1995 Q1	93 938	22 149	541	184	33 104	149 916	2 200		
Q2	93 840	21 866	1 383	122	33 529	150 740	1 715		
Q3	94 167	22 910	1 462	119	34 027	152 685	704		
Q4	95 950	24 102	1 248	188	34 512	156 000	283		
1996 Q1	97 374	23 145	587	78	34 843	156 027	1 238		
Seasonally adjusted									
1992 Q1	84 544	13 815	518	18	27 684	126 579	629	-	**125 950**
Q2	85 381	15 798	628	36	28 190	130 033	261	-	**129 772**
Q3	85 877	15 934	581	96	28 721	131 209	317	-	**130 892**
Q4	86 213	16 309	634	56	28 877	132 089	571	-	**131 518**
1993 Q1	87 015	16 961	1 114	8	29 558	134 656	1 005	-	**133 651**
Q2	87 674	18 089	751	74	29 712	136 300	326	-	**135 974**
Q3	88 549	19 964	682	54	30 218	139 467	541	-	**138 926**
Q4	88 581	19 806	907	57	30 601	139 952	478	-	**139 474**
1994 Q1	89 814	20 513	622	212	31 049	142 210	286	-	**141 924**
Q2	90 735	21 079	1 148	82	31 494	144 538	842	-	**143 696**
Q3	91 896	22 341	1 211	94	32 049	147 591	1 286	-	**146 305**
Q4	92 501	22 535	1 249	102	32 485	148 872	1 620	-	**147 252**
1995 Q1	93 516	22 605	1 083	184	33 148	150 536	1 709	-34	**148 793**
Q2	94 155	23 515	1 121	122	33 496	152 409	1 636	-44	**150 729**
Q3	94 485	22 938	1 385	119	34 011	152 938	1 225	-49	**151 664**
Q4	95 739	21 969	1 045	188	34 517	153 458	332	-53	**153 073**
1996 Q1	97 056	22 569	985	78	34 887	155 575	956	-46	**154 573**
Percentage change, latest year on previous year									
1995	3.5	5.3	9.6	6.4	4.5			4.3	
Percentage change, latest quarter on previous quarter									
1996 Q1	1.4	2.7	-5.7	1.1	1.4			1.0	
Percentage change, latest quarter on corresponding quarter of previous year									
1996 Q1	3.8	-0.2	-9.0	5.2	3.3			3.9	

1 Estimates are given to the nearest £ million but cannot be regarded as accurate to this degree.
2. Quarterly alignment adjustment included in this series.
3. Before providing for depreciation and stock appreciation.
4. Including financial institutions.
5. Figures reflect privatisations.
6. Income from rent and from self-employment, and the imputed charge for the consumption of non-trading capital.
7. The sum of the factor incomes before deducting Stock appreciation.

Source: Office for National Statistics

From: UK Economic Accounts 1996 Q1, Table A3

4.6 Index numbers of output at constant factor cost[1]

1990 = 100

		Production					Service industries					Gross domestic product at factor cost[2]	Gross domestic product excl. oil and gas extraction
	Agriculture, forestry and fishing	Mining & quarrying inc oil and gas extraction	Manufacturing (revised definition)	Electricity gas and water supply	Total	Construction	Distribution hotels and catering; repairs	Transport storage and communication	Financial and business services	Government and other services	Total		
1990 Weights[3]	19	24	232	22	278	72	143	84	193	212	631	**1000**	983
1988	92.1	120.9	95.9	97.7	98.2	92.3	97.8	94.6	96.0	98.8	97.2	**97.3**	96.8
1989	96.7	104.0	100.2	97.3	100.3	97.6	101.2	99.2	97.6	99.4	99.2	**99.4**	99.4
1990	100.0	100.0	100.0	100.0	100.0	100.0	100.0	100.0	100.0	100.0	100.0	**100.0**	100.0
1991	101.5	104.5	94.6	105.7	96.3	92.0	96.1	98.2	99.7	100.8	99.1	**97.9**	97.8
1992	106.0	107.8	94.0	107.4	96.2	87.9	95.2	99.8	98.1	101.4	98.8	**97.4**	97.1
1993	98.2	115.2	95.3	111.8	98.3	87.2	99.9	104.8	100.7	102.5	101.6	**99.6**	99.1
1994	98.0	132.4	99.3	113.1	103.2	90.5	103.4	112.2	105.3	103.8	105.3	**103.7**	102.7
1995	98.6	139.3	101.5	116.7	105.9	89.6	104.5	118.5	110.2	105.3	108.4	**106.2**	105.2
Seasonally adjusted													
1992 Q1	104.1	107.6	93.7	105.6	95.9	88.8	94.2	99.1	97.4	101.1	98.1	**96.9**	96.7
Q2	105.3	103.3	94.0	104.0	95.6	87.9	95.2	99.4	97.7	101.3	98.6	**97.1**	96.9
Q3	108.0	108.1	94.0	108.4	96.4	87.9	95.5	99.7	98.7	101.4	99.0	**97.6**	97.3
Q4	106.5	112.4	94.2	111.6	97.2	87.0	96.1	100.8	98.7	101.7	99.4	**98.0**	97.5
1993 Q1	100.8	107.9	95.1	105.3	97.0	86.7	98.5	102.2	99.5	102.4	100.6	**98.6**	98.3
Q2	95.1	109.3	95.1	109.7	97.5	86.6	99.8	103.8	100.4	102.2	101.3	**99.1**	98.7
Q3	98.5	118.5	95.3	114.7	98.8	86.9	100.7	106.0	101.2	102.4	102.1	**100.1**	99.5
Q4	98.3	125.1	95.9	117.4	100.0	88.4	100.5	107.0	101.7	102.8	102.5	**100.8**	100.0
1994 Q1	98.0	127.9	97.3	109.5	100.8	89.5	101.9	109.8	103.0	103.4	103.8	**102.0**	101.1
Q2	98.0	134.4	98.9	114.0	103.1	90.5	102.8	111.3	104.3	103.8	104.7	**103.3**	102.3
Q3	97.4	134.2	100.2	118.3	104.5	90.7	104.3	112.4	105.8	104.0	105.7	**104.3**	103.3
Q4	98.7	133.2	101.0	110.6	104.5	91.6	104.7	115.3	107.9	104.2	106.9	**105.1**	104.1
1995 Q1	98.6	140.7	100.7	114.8	105.2	90.2	104.2	116.4	108.9	104.5	107.4	**105.5**	104.3
Q2	101.4	136.0	101.5	116.5	105.6	89.5	104.4	117.8	109.3	105.1	107.9	**105.9**	104.9
Q3	98.5	140.3	102.0	117.3	106.4	89.1	104.3	119.3	110.8	105.6	108.7	**106.6**	105.5
Q4	95.9	140.2	101.8	118.0	106.3	89.6	105.2	120.5	111.7	106.0	109.5	**107.0**	105.9
1996 Q1	99.3	141.6	101.5	121.8	106.6	89.2	105.1	121.5	112.3	106.6	110.0	**107.4**	106.3
Percentage change, latest year on previous year													
1995	0.6					-1.0	1.1	5.6	4.7	1.4	2.9	2.5	2.4
Percentage change, latest quarter on previous quarter													
1996 Q1	3.6	1.0	-0.2	3.2	0.2	-0.4	-0.1	0.8	0.6	0.5	0.5	0.4	0.4
Percentage change, latest quarter on corresponding quarter of previous year													
1996 Q1	0.8	0.6	0.8	6.1	1.2	-1.1	0.9	4.4	3.2	2.0	2.5	1.9	1.9

1 Estimates cannot be regarded as accurate to the last digit shown.
2 Embraces an implicit statistical descrepancy compared with the sum of the previous columns, because GDP takes account of other information based on incomes and expenditures.
3 Weights may not sum to the totals due to rounding.

Source: Office for National Statistics

From: UK Economic Accounts 1996 Q1, Table A4

KEEPING TRACK OF THE ECONOMY

.....is easier with Economic Trends, the Office for National Statistics flagship monthly which brings together all the key economic indicators.

At £21 it is an essential reference guide for anyone who needs to keep abreast of economic statistics.

- national accounts
- employment
- prices
- goverment finance
- investment
- earnings
- trade
- bank lending

Statistics and graphs cover these and many other areas for the last 5 years or more.

There is also a monthly analysis of indicators and the business cycle over the last 20 years, surveys of international and regional economic indicators and regular articles offering in-depth commentary on important areas of economic statistics.

A companion quarterly publication, *UK Economic Accounts,* price £21, offers up-to-date analyis of the national and financial accounts and the balance of payments.

Available from the ONS Sales Desk on 0171-270 6081 or from HMSO.

ECONOMIC TRENDS

Published for the Office for National Statistics by HMSO.
Price £21
ISSN 0013 0400
(Annual subscription including the Annual Supplement, UK Economic Accounts and postage £335)

five

UK finance

Definitions and sources

A new presentation of the measure of broad money was introduced in May 1987. Among other changes, M4 was introduced to cover the sterling deposit liabilities of banks and building societies for the rest of the private sector, and holdings by the latter of notes and coin.

The public sector borrowing requirement (PSBR) indicates the extent to which the public sector borrows from other sectors of the economy and overseas to finance the balance of expenditure and receipts arising from its various activities.

A much wider range of financial series is shown in *Financial Statistics* monthly and the *Bank of England Quarterly Bulletin*. More detailed information is given in the supplementary notes to the *Monthly Digest of Statistics* and in the *Financial Statistics Explanatory Handbook*.

For other sources see: *Guide to Official Statistics, 1996 edition* (520 pages approximately, fully indexed) HMSO.

Financial Statistics, HMSO.

5.1 Monetary aggregates

£ million

	Amount outstanding					
	'Narrow' money		'Broad' money			
	M0-the wide monetary base		Retail deposits and cash in M4		M4	
	Not seasonally adjusted	Seasonally adjusted	Not seasonally adjusted	Seasonally adjusted	Not seasonally adjusted	Seasonally adjusted
1991	20 085	18 857	335 928	334 870	503 824	503 427
1992	20 581	19 393	373 243	372 367	517 400	517 299
1993	21 729	20 558	394 510	393 776	543 453	543 280
1994	23 322	21 945	410 469	409 672	565 851	565 597
1995	24 539	23 201	436 914	436 118	622 931	622 203
1993 Q4	21 729	20 558	394 510	393 776	543 453	543 280
1994 Q1	20 564	20 806	400 933	398 920	553 725	550 286
Q2	21 163	21 190	401 279	399 992	557 151	554 320
Q3	21 610	21 614	404 666	404 285	559 621	559 775
Q4	23 322	21 945	410 469	409 672	565 851	565 597
1995 Q1	21 880	22 266	417 202	415 290	582 846	578 986
Q2	22 266	22 386	424 328	422 796	594 486	591 579
Q3	22 798	22 797	430 782	429 863	605 293	605 782
Q4	24 539	23 201	436 914	436 118	622 931	622 203
1996 Q1	23 124	23 474	445 242	443 418	639 992	636 163
1995 Feb	21 549	22 025	411 214	413 639	568 586	573 211
Mar	21 880	22 266	417 202	415 290	582 846	578 986
Apr	22 503	22 377	420 519	418 353	582 705	581 203
May	22 360	22 338	421 499	420 049	588 632	586 571
Jun	22 266	22 386	424 328	422 796	594 486	591 579
Jul	22 632	22 536	425 898	425 734	601 015	598 585
Aug	22 971	22 683	426 860	427 410	603 080	603 010
Sep	22 798	22 797	430 782	429 863	605 293	605 782
Oct	22 728	22 860	430 906	431 633	607 597	610 378
Nov	22 940	22 985	433 622	434 196	615 070	616 410
Dec	24 539	23 201	436 914	436 118	622 931	622 203
1996 Jan	23 160	23 148	433 753	437 776	624 563	628 688
Feb	22 877	23 358	436 864	439 795	627 254	632 066
Mar	23 124	23 474	445 242	443 418	639 992	636 163

1 Equals M2 from December 1992.

Source: Bank of England

From: Monthly Digest of Statistics, May 1996, Table 17.4

5.2 Public sector borrowing requirement

£ million

	Total			Contributions by:			Financed by: Banks and building societies/ Overseas sector — External finance			Other private sector	
	PSBR excluding privatisation proceeds	Not seasonally adjusted	Seasonally adjusted[1]	Central government (own account)[2]	Local authorities[3]	Public corporations[3]	Borrowing in sterling from banks	Foreign currency borrowing from banks	Other external finance	Notes and coin	Other
1993	47 882	42 503	43 671	46 255	-2 875	-877	4 492	387	12 862	1 028	..
1994	44 347	37 888	38 273	38 649	167	-928	9 062	-4 098	5 314	1 148	..
1995	38 022	35 486	35 272	36 238	370	-1 122	8 452	90	2 876	1 332	..
Financial years											
1993/94	50 849	45 419	45 419	48 101	-2 781	99	6 554	-3 309	15 477	2 267	..
1994/95	42 330	35 897	35 897	38 277	-964	-1 416	7 557	-753	783	473	..
1995/96	34 578	32 143	32 143	35 528	-701	-2 684	..	..	..	..	..
1994 Q4	5 958	3 749	8 082	4 564	-1	-814	683	-246	-257	706	..
1995 Q1	14 014	12 082	10 023	11 851	-174	405	3 284	66	-1 938	-293	..
Q2	11 338	11 325	8 629	10 990	734	-399	4 668	-288	3 194	359	..
Q3	8 720	8 733	8 712	9 785	-447	-605	3 721	478	947	140	..
Q4	3 950	3 346	7 908	3 612	257	-523	-3 221	-166	673	1 126	..
1996 Q1	10 570	8 739	6 894	11 141	-1 245	-1 157	..	..	..	..	..

1 Financial year constrained.
2 An increase in debt is shown positive.
3 Incudes direct borrowing from central government.

Source: Office for National Statistics

From: Monthly Digest of Statistics, May 1996, Table 17.2

5.3 Selected interest rates, exchange rates and security prices

£ million

	Selected retail banks' base rate	Average discount rate for 91 day Treasury bills	Inter bank 3 months bid rate	Inter bank 3 months offer rate	British government securities 20 years yield[1]	Exchange rate US spot	Ordinary share price index[2]
1994 Oct	5.75	5.43	5.91	5.97	8.63	1.6306	1 516.65
Nov	5.75	5.72	5.97	6.00	8.53	1.5653	1 533.46
Dec	6.25	5.92	6.53	6.56	8.44	1.5645	1 502.42
1995 Jan	6.25	6.11	6.69	6.72	8.61	1.5870	1 501.87
Feb	6.75	6.19	6.69	6.75	8.52	1.5807	1 506.17
Mar	6.75	6.11	6.59	6.63	8.50	1.6280	1 511.04
Apr	6.75	6.61	6.91	6.94	8.39	1.6097	1 566.98
May	6.75	6.08	6.50	6.56	8.18	1.5897	1 614.69
Jun	6.75	6.62	6.88	6.91	8.16	1.5908	1 643.59
Jul	6.75	6.60	6.78	6.81	8.36	1.6010	1 680.80
Aug	6.75	6.57	6.75	6.78	8.24	1.5490	1 718.13
Sep	6.75	6.54	6.75	6.78	8.09	1.5825	1 743.26
Oct	6.75	6.53	6.69	6.72	8.29	1.5809	1 739.84
Nov	6.75	6.38	6.59	6.63	7.97	1.5290	1 755.17
Dec	6.50	6.22	6.47	6.50	7.75	1.5505	1 783.30
1996 Jan	6.25	6.01	6.22	6.25	7.79	1.5110	1 818.72
Feb	6.25	5.93	6.13	6.16	8.10	1.5312	1 839.78
Mar	6.00	5.80	6.00	6.06	8.34	1.5262	1 836 04
Apr	6.00	5.79	5.97	6.00	8.30	1.5000	1 892.47

1 Average of working day.
2 *Financial Times* Actuaries share indices 10 April 1962 = 100. All classes (750 shares) index.

Source: Bank of England

From: Monthly Digest of Statistics, May 1996, Table 17.5

5.4 Selected financial statistics

£ million

| | National savings[1] | Building societies | | Unit trusts | Net inflow into life assurance & super-annuation funds |
| | | Advances | | | |
		Not seasonally adjusted	Seasonally adjusted		
Amount outstanding					
31 Dec 1995	55 922	240 930		112 624	
Transactions					
1992	5 147	14 746	14 874	648	28 556
1993	3 117	11 162	11 371	9 096	29 549
1994	4 697	14 372	14 502	8 344	27 977
1995	3 427	16 041	16 056	6 921	30 657
1995 Q1	741	4 256	4 448	638	7 230
Q2	728	3 753	3 805	1 682	5 790
Q3	595	4 740	4 072	2 737	8 904
Q4	1 363	3 292	3 731	1 864	9 543
1996 Q1	2 582	3 234	3 409	..	..
1995 Jun	265	1 449	1 342	634	..
Jul	141	2 570	1 850	1 298	..
Aug	227	903	1 067	787	..
Sep	227	1 267	1 155	652	..
Oct	426	1 280	1 368	600	..
Nov	421	973	1 059	612	..
Dec	516	1 039	1 304	652	..
1996 Jan	1 095	1 263	1 487	1 348	..
Feb	748	626	882	819	..
Mar	739	1 345	1 040	..	..

1 Total administered by the Department for National Savings.
2 Monthly figures relate to calendar months.

Source: Office for National Statistics; Department for National Savings; Building Societies Commission; Association of Unit Trusts and Investment Funds; Bank of England; Department of Trade and Industry

From: Monthly Digest of Statistics, May 1996, Table 17.3

(continued overleaf)

5.4 Selected financial statistics
continued

	Banks[2]						Consumer credit		of which Credit cards	
	Uk private sector deposits			Lending to the private sector						
	Sterling			Sterling						
	Not seasonally adjusted	Seasonally adjusted	Other currencies	Not seasonally adjusted	Seasonally adjusted	Other currencies	Not seasonally adjusted	Seasonally adjusted	Not seasonally adjusted	Seasonally adjusted
Amount outstanding										
31 Dec 1995	411 809		94 526	490 458		109 883	65 108	64 642	13 836	13 293
Transactions							Net lending	Net lending	Net lending	Net lending
1992	4 220		6 660	9 075		-2 668	464	476	134	115
1993	14 873		5 868	12 387		7 654	2 655	2 766	719	704
1994	12 652		10 899	21 180		7 053	5 742	5 678	1 483	1 418
1995	42 235		12 384	44 141		6 100	7 761	7 666	2 107	2 057
1995 Q1	16 983	12 506	3 617	13 719	10 341	5 822	1 180	1 775	-295	445
Q2	5 997	8 149	1 399	5 274	9 660	-2 781	1 773	1 698	766	508
Q3	4 615	8 274	4 765	9 415	9 888	1 433	2 349	1 951	514	478
Q4	14 640	13 332	2 603	15 733	14 516	1 626	2 459	2 242	1 122	626
1996 Q1	14 932	10 429	10 284	18 781	15 138	7 349	1 287	1 973	-311	478
1995 Jun	2 379	..	1 066	356	..	-1 089	858	579	272	102
Jul	4 231	..	1 014	4 970	..	-2 243	566	728	91	159
Aug	-513	..	1 980	-680	..	4 111	790	580	115	125
Sep	896	..	1 772	5 125	..	-435	993	643	308	194
Oct	1 412	..	1 890	2 919	..	-3 355	586	843	74	244
Nov	8 294	..	-423	4 964	..	1 831	625	603	266	151
Dec	4 934	..	1 136	7 849	..	3 151	1 248	796	781	230
1996 Jan	1 505	..	8 588	5 860	..	9 341	310	572	-118	148
Feb	1 277	..	5 381	4 464	..	-785	137	701	-268	159
Mar	12 150	..	-3 685	8 457	..	-1 207	840	700	74	170

1 Total administered by the Department for National Savings.
2 Monthly figures relate to calendar months.

Source: Office for National Statistics; Department for National Savings; Building Societies Commission; Association of Unit Trusts and Investment Funds; Bank of England; Department of Trade and Industry

From: Monthly Digest of Statistics, May 1996, Table 17.3

six

Balance of payments

Definitions and sources

The object of the balance of payments accounts is to identify and record transactions between residents of the United Kingdom and residents overseas (non-residents) in a way that is suitable for analysing the economic relations between the UK economy and the rest of the world. In the UK balance of payments accounts, transactions are classified into main groups as follows:

Current account transactions cover exports and imports of goods and services, investment income and most transfers.

Transactions in UK external assets and liabilities cover inward and outward investment, transactions by banks in the United Kingdom, borrowing and lending overseas by other UK residents, drawings on and accruals to the official reserves, and other capital transactions.

The *current balance* shows whether the United Kingdom has had a surplus of income over expenditure; and, taken with capital transfers, it shows whether the United Kingdom has added to or consumed its net external assets in any period.

In concept every balance of payments transaction involves equal credit and debit entries, relating to the two halves of the transaction so that the accounts are analogous to a double-entry book-keeping system. For example an export of goods, recorded as positive, would be matched by a negative entry, which could be one of the following:

    (i)   an increase in the foreign assets (claims on non-residents) of the United Kingdom (eg an increase in UK residents' deposits with banks abroad);

    (ii) a decrease in the United Kingdom's liabilities to non-residents (eg a fall in sterling deposits with UK banks);

  or (iii) in the case of a barter transaction, by imports of similar value

Conversely imports of goods, recorded as negative, are likely to be matched by positive entries representing reductions in foreign assets held by the United Kingdom or increases in the United Kingdom's liabilities to non-residents.

Since the two entries made in respect of each transaction generally derived from separate sources and methods of estimation are neither complete nor precisely accurate, the two entries may not match each other precisely or may fall within different recording periods. In order to bring the total of all entries to zero an additional entry, the balancing item, is therefore included to reflect the sum of all these errors and omissions. The balancing item will include persistent elements, where certain types of transactions are not adequately covered in the accounts, and timing differences.

The balance of payments estimates are compiled from a large number of different sources and the degree of accuracy attained varies considerably between items. Errors are likely, to some extent, to offset each other in any particular year but where a balance is drawn between two aggregates and the balance is small in relation to the aggregates, such as the current balance, the proportionate error attached to the balance is liable to be very substantial.

Detailed notes and definitions relating to the balance of payments (including foreign trade) are given in the annual publication *United Kingdom Balance of Payments (the ONS 'Pink Book')*.

The data in these tables are consistent with that published in the June 1996 Balance of Payments First Release. The 1996 edition of the *Pink Book*, due to be published on 2 August, will be consistent with this publication and with the June 1996 Balance of Payments First Release.

For other sources see: Guide to Official Statistics, 1996 edition (520 pages approximately, fully indexed) HMSO.

UK Balance of Payments, ONS 'Pink Book'.

Overseas Trade Statistics of the United Kingdom.

6.1 Summary of balance of payments

£ million

	1985	1986	1987	1988	1989	1990	1991	1992	1993	1994	1995
Current account (balances)											
Trade in goods	-3 345	-9 559	-11 582	-21 480	-24 683	-18 809	-10 284	-13 104	-13 460	-10 831	-11 628
Trade in services	6 398	6 223	6 242	3 957	3 361	3 689	3 564	4 950	5 516	4 747	6 142
Trade in goods and services	3 053	-3 336	-5 340	-17 523	-21 322	-15 120	-6 720	-8 154	-7 944	-6 084	-5 486
Investment income	2 296	4 629	3 927	4 566	3 502	1 269	150	3 124	2 197	8 691	9 572
Transfers balance	-3 111	-2 157	-3 400	-3 518	-4 578	-4 896	-1 383	-5 102	-5 007	-5 027	-6 978
Current balance	2 238	-864	-4 813	-16 475	-22 398	-18 746	-7 954	-10 133	-10 756	-2 419	-2 892
Capital transfers	-	-	-	-	-	-	-	-	-	-	-
Transactions in UK assets and liabilities											
UK external assets	-50 617	-91 693	-82 722	-57 495	-90 668	-80 415	-18 683	-81 600	-155 611	-35 147	-124 045
UK external liabilities	46 897	87 874	90 132	72 412	108 844	96 958	26 128	86 565	168 691	32 497	124 491
Net transactions	-3 720	-3 820	7 410	14 917	18 176	16 543	7 445	4 965	13 080	-2 650	446
EEA loss on forward commitments	-	-	-	-	-	-	-	-	-	-	-
Allocation of special drawing rights	-	-	-	-	-	-	-	-	-	-	-
Gold subscription to IMF	-	-	-	-	-	-	-	-	-	-	-
Balancing item	1 482	4 684	-2 597	1 558	4 222	2 203	509	5 168	-2 324	5 069	2 446

Source: Office for National Statistics

From: UK Balance of Payments 1996, Table 1.1

6.2 Current account

£ million

	1985	1986	1987	1988	1989	1990	1991	1992	1993	1994	1995
Credits											
Exports of goods (f.o.b.)	77 991	72 627	79 153	80 346	92 154	101 718	103 413	107 343	121 398	134 666	152 346
Exports of services											
General government	483	511	521	550	445	425	457	441	540	543	481
Private sector and public corporations											
Sea transport	2 986	2 859	2 932	3 276	3 522	3 444	3 351	3 525	3 913	4 246	4 550
Civil aviation	3 078	2 786	3 159	3 292	3 869	4 474	4 039	4 512	5 144	5 461	5 931
Travel	5 442	5 553	6 260	6 184	6 945	7 785	7 168	8 076	9 487	9 920	11 906
Financial and allied institutions (net credits)	4 207	5 429	5 927	4 825	4 183	3 899	3 961	4 612	5 221	5 424	5 778
Other business services	7 854	8 120	8 445	8 800	10 368	11 420	11 900	13 605	14 294	15 805	16 608
Total goods and services	102 041	97 885	106 397	107 273	121 486	133 165	134 289	142 114	159 997	176 065	197 600
Investment income											
General government	738	765	949	1 460	1 949	1 812	1 754	1 568	1 413	1 610	1 641
Private sector and public corporations	51 272	46 576	47 053	55 090	72 029	77 294	75 213	66 984	72 731	76 309	91 498
Transfers											
General government	1 760	2 138	2 282	2 115	2 143	2 232	4 899	2 888	3 325	3 296	3 697
Private sector	1 775	1 732	1 666	1 715	1 750	1 800	1 900	1 957	2 211	2 322	2 438
Total credits	157 584	149 096	158 347	167 653	199 357	216 303	218 055	215 510	239 676	259 602	296 874
Debits											
Imports of goods (f.o.b.)	81 336	82 186	90 735	101 826	116 837	120 527	113 697	120 447	134 858	145 497	163 974
Imports of services											
General government	1 781	1 920	2 141	2 351	2 699	2 784	2 808	2 546	2 332	2 523	2 501
Private sector and public corporations											
Sea transport	3 515	3 323	3 219	3 517	3 779	3 756	3 634	3 821	4 225	4 561	4 715
Civil aviation	2 877	3 194	3 775	4 203	4 397	4 769	4 423	5 048	5 413	6 125	6 272
Travel	4 871	6 083	7 280	8 216	9 357	9 916	9 834	11 283	12 972	14 500	15 609
Other business services	4 608	4 515	4 587	4 683	5 739	6 533	6 613	7 123	8 141	8 943	10 015
Total goods and services	98 988	101 221	111 737	124 796	142 808	148 285	141 009	150 268	167 941	182 149	203 086
Investment income											
General government	1 492	1 672	1 875	2 181	2 538	2 765	2 620	3 178	3 329	4 035	4 360
Private sector and public corporations	48 220	41 040	42 200	49 803	67 938	75 072	74 197	62 249	68 617	65 193	79 207
Transfers											
General government	5 187	4 371	5 559	5 363	6 421	6 828	5 982	7 722	8 294	8 431	10 877
Private sector	1 459	1 656	1 789	1 985	2 050	2 100	2 200	2 225	2 249	2 214	2 236
Total debits	155 346	149 960	163 160	184 128	221 755	235 050	226 008	225 642	250 430	262 022	299 766
Balances											
Trade in goods	-3 345	-9 559	-11 582	-21 480	-24 683	-18 809	-10 284	-13 104	-13 460	-10 831	-11 628
Trade in services											
General government	-1 298	-1 409	-1 620	-1 801	-2 254	-2 359	-2 351	-2 105	-1 792	-1 980	-2 020
Private sector and public corporations											
Sea transport	-529	-464	-287	-241	-257	-312	-283	-296	-312	-315	-165
Civil aviation	201	-408	-616	-911	-528	-295	-384	-536	-269	-664	-341
Travel	571	-530	-1 020	-2 032	-2 412	-2 131	-2 666	-3 207	-3 485	-4 580	-3 703
Financial and other services	7 453	9 034	9 785	8 942	8 812	8 786	9 248	11 094	11 374	12 286	12 371
Total goods and services	3 053	-3 336	-5 340	-17 523	-21 322	-15 120	-6 720	-8 154	-7 944	-6 084	-5 486
Investment income											
General government	-754	-907	-926	-721	-589	-953	-866	-1 610	-1 916	-2 425	-2 719
Private sector and public corporations	3 052	5 536	4 853	5 287	4 091	2 222	1 016	4 735	4 114	11 116	12 291
Transfers											
General government	-3 427	-2 233	-3 277	-3 248	-4 278	-4 596	-1 083	-4 834	-4 969	-5 135	-7 180
Private sector	316	76	-123	-270	-300	-300	-300	-268	-38	108	202
Currrent balance	2 238	-864	-4 813	-16 475	-22 398	-18 746	-7 954	-10 133	-10 756	-2 419	-2 892

Source: Office for National Statistics

From: UK Balance of Payments 1996, Table 1.3

6.3 Summary of levels of identified UK external assets and liabilities
(Balance sheet of the United Kingdom with the overseas sector)
End of period

£ billion

	1985	1986	1987	1988	1989	1990	1991	1992	1993	1994	1995
External assets of the UK											
Direct investment overseas by UK residents	69.4	80.7	85.3	103.7	122.4	119.7	125.3	148.4	169.2	179.5	213.8
Portfolio investment in overseas securities by UK residents	99.4	140.1	112.9	145.6	215.2	189.6	240.9	303.0	438.4	401.6	481.9
Lending etc to overseas residents by UK banks	369.6	438.2	425.2	447.9	521.5	498.5	460.5	565.9	562.0	604.2	682.0
Deposits and lending overseas by UK residents other than banks and general government											
Assets with banks abroad	23.4	27.3	28.7	32.9	49.0	53.8	58.3	74.4	85.4	95.2	108.6
Other assets	10.0	8.2	7.3	6.6	12.8	16.4	26.4	43.5	89.6	64.3	84.9
Official reserves	13.2	17.4	27.0	28.7	26.3	22.5	26.0	28.3	29.7	30.7	31.8
Other external assets of central government	8.4	9.0	8.7	9.3	9.7	10.9	12.0	13.3	13.7	13.5	13.9
Total assets of											
General government	21.6	26.4	35.7	38.0	36.0	33.3	37.9	41.6	43.5	44.2	45.7
Public corporations	0.8	0.9	0.8	0.7	0.8	0.8	0.9	1.0	1.0	1.1	1.3
UK banks	398.8	476.1	457.9	481.3	565.6	544.7	515.2	644.0	677.1	731.6	836.8
UK non-banks private sector	172.4	217.3	200.7	254.5	354.6	332.4	395.3	490.3	666.4	612.1	733.2
Total	593.6	720.8	695.1	774.6	957.0	911.3	949.3	1 176.8	1 388.0	1 388.9	1 617.0
UK liabilities to overseas residents											
Direct investment in the UK by overseas residents	44.3	51.7	62.6	76.8	99.8	113.2	120.7	122.7	127.9	129.6	150.4
Portfolio investment in the UK by overseas residents	33.0	49.0	67.9	86.6	110.7	109.6	135.0	181.9	256.3	266.9	308.9
Borrowing etc from overseas residents by UK banks	416.0	484.4	466.0	503.5	603.0	584.5	556.6	670.5	691.7	738.1	836.9
Borrowing from overseas by UK residents other than banks and general government											
Liabilities to banks abroad	19.9	24.5	23.8	27.1	42.0	48.7	62.2	77.6	99.8	98.1	132.0
Other liabilities	5.5	6.8	7.5	10.1	30.3	37.8	55.5	92.6	168.9	115.8	130.4
Other external liabilities of general government	4.0	4.7	6.2	7.1	10.3	10.7	8.4	9.3	6.2	6.7	8.6
Total liabilities of											
General government	16.2	20.2	25.2	26.9	28.1	28.1	34.1	46.5	64.3	63.3	68.0
Public corporations	4.0	4.1	3.1	2.8	1.2	0.9	0.9	0.4	0.3	0.5	0.4
UK private sector	502.5	596.9	605.7	681.5	866.9	875.3	903.4	1 107.6	1 286.1	1 291.2	1 498.7
Total	522.7	621.1	634.0	711.2	896.1	904.4	938.4	1 154.5	1 350.7	1 355.1	1 567.1
Of which identified liabilities constituting overseas authorities exchange reserves in sterling	9.3	9.6	13.9	16.1	16.8	17.9	16.7	18.6	24.7	22.3	24.4
Net identified UK external assets and liabilities											
Direct investment	25.1	28.9	22.7	26.8	22.6	6.5	4.6	25.7	41.3	50.0	63.4
Portfolio investment	66.3	91.1	44.9	59.0	104.5	80.0	105.9	121.1	182.1	134.7	173.0
Lending and borrowing by UK banks	-46.1	-46.2	-40.8	-55.6	-81.5	-85.9	-96.1	-104.6	-129.7	-133.9	-154.9
Lending and borrowing by UK residents other than banks and general government	8.0	4.2	4.8	2.3	-10.4	-16.3	-33.0	-52.2	-93.7	-54.3	-68.8
Other assets and liabilities of general government	17.6	21.7	29.5	30.9	25.7	22.6	29.6	32.3	37.3	37.4	37.1
Net identified assets of:											
General government	5.4	6.3	10.5	11.1	8.0	5.2	3.9	-4.9	-20.8	-19.2	-22.3
Public corporations	-3.2	-3.2	-2.3	-2.0	-0.4	-0.1	-	0.6	0.7	0.6	0.9
UK private sector	68.7	96.6	52.9	54.4	53.4	1.8	7.0	26.6	57.4	52.4	71.3
Total net	71.0	99.7	61.1	63.4	60.9	6.9	10.9	22.3	37.3	33.9	49.9
Allocations of Special Drawing Rights to the UK by the IMF	1.5	1.6	1.5	1.4	1.6	1.4	1.5	1.7	1.8	1.8	1.8

Source: Office for National Statistics

From: UK Balance of Payments 1996, Table 7.1

seven

European Community

Definitions and sources

As a European power, Britain is concerned first of all with the prosperity and security of this area of the world.

The main instrument for achieving European prosperity is the European Union (EU), an association of 12 democratic nations - Belgium, Britain, Denmark, France, Germany, Greece, the Irish Republic, Italy, Luxembourg, the Netherlands, Portugal and Spain.

Negotiations on an Accession Treaty for Austria, Finland, Norway and Sweden were completed in April 1994 and they signed the Treaty in June 1994 at the Corfu European Council meeting. Austria held a referendum on 12 June 1994, and voters supported accession. The other three countries held referendums in the autumn of 1994.

Britain regards the Union as a means of strengthening democracy and reinforcing political stability in Europe, and of increasing the collective strength of member states in international negotiations. The Government wants Britain to be at the heart of a Union in which member states work effectively together by pooling their ideas and resources for shared purposes, provided that such objectives cannot be achieved by member states acting on their own.

The Union had its origins in the post-World War II resolve by Western European nations, particularly France and Germany, not to allow wars to break out again between themselves. The 1957 Rome Treaty, which established the European Community (EC-now part of the European Union), defined its aims as a harmonious development of economic activities, a continuous and balanced economic expansion and an accelerated rise in the standard of living. These objectives were to be achieved by the creation of a common internal market and progressive harmonisation of economic policies, involving:

- the elimination of customs duties between member states;
- free movement of goods, people, services and capital;
- a common commercial policy towards other countries;
- the elimination of distortions in competition within the common market;
- the creation of a Social Fund to improve job opportunities for workers and raise their standard of living;
- the adoption of common agriculture and transport policies; and
- the association of overseas developing countries with the community in order to increase trade and promote economic and social development.

These objectives were confirmed and augmented by the Single European Act of 1986 and the 1992 Maastricht Treaty on European Union.

Maastricht Treaty

The Maastricht Treaty amends the Rome Treaty and makes other new commitments. It:

- introduces the concept of European Union citizenship, as a supplement to national citizenship, provides some measure of institutional reform, and strengthens control of the Community's finances;

- provides on an intergovernmental basis for a common foreign and security policy and for greater co-operation on issues concerned with interior/justice policy;

- clarifies and codifies Union competencies in areas such as regional strategy, consumer protection, education and vocational training, the environment and public health;

- provides for moves towards economic and monetary union;and embodies the principle of subsidiarity under which action is taken by the European Union only if its objectives cannot be achieved by member states acting alone.

- provides for moves towards economic and monetary union;and

- embodies the principle of subsidiarity under which action is taken by the European Union only if its objectives cannot be achieved by member states acting alone.

Under an agreement reached in 1992 a subsidiarity test is applied to all European Commission proposals for action.

The Treaty was ratified by Britain and the other member states and came into force in November 1993.

Economic and Monetary Union

During the negotiations on economic and monetary union (EMU), the Government sought to ensure that:

- there would be no commitment by Britain to move to a single monetary policy or single currency;
- monetary matters would remain a national responsibility until the Union moved to a single currency and monetary policy;
- member states would retain primary responsibility for their economic policies; and
- there were clear and quantifiable convergence conditions which member states would have to satisfy before moving to a single currency.

The Maastricht Treaty provides for progress towards EMU in three stages: the first-completion of the single market-ended at the end of 1993. The second stage, which began on 1 January 1994, includes the establishment of a European Monetary Institute with a largely advisory and consultative role. Although the Institute will prepare for stage 3, monetary policy will still be a national responsibility. Member states will co-ordinate economic policies in the context of agreed non-binding policy guidelines. The British Government is participating in Stage 2.

Under the Treaty a single currency is envisaged by 1 January 1999, although member states will have to satisfy certain criteria on inflation rates, government deficit levels, currency fluctuation margins and interest rates. A special protocol recognises that Britain is not obliged or committed to move to this final stage of EMU without a separate decision to do so by the Government and Parliament at the appropriate time.

The Community Budget

The Community's revenue consists of:

- levies on agricultural imports; customs duties;
- the proceeds of a notional rate of value added tax of up to 1.4 per cent on a standard basket of goods and services; and
- contributions from member states based on gross national product (GNP).

Overall revenue is limited by a ceiling of 1.2 per cent of Union GNP. Britain has an annual rebate worth some £2,000 million because of the fact that, without it, British net contributions would be far greater than that justified by its share of Union GNP.

 Key Data 96, © Crown copyright 1996

An agreement on future finance was reached at the 1992 Edinburgh summit. Under this the revenue ceiling will remain at 1.2 per cent until 1995, when it will rise in steps, reaching 1.27 per cent of Union GNP in 1999. Agriculture spending will be less than half the budget by the end of the century, compared with 80 per cent in 1973 and 60 per cent at present. It was also agreed that more resources would be allocated to the poorer regions of the Union.

Single Market

The single market has been completed in several essential respects. It covers, among other things, the liberalisation of capital movements, the opening of up of public procurement markets and the mutual recognition of professional qualifications. It is designed to reduce business costs, stimulate efficiency and encourage the creation of jobs and wealth. The British Government is supporting continuing work on extending the single market to important areas such as telecommunications and energy.

Transport

Britain fully supports the liberalisation of transport in the Union. Considerable progress has been made so far. Permits and quotas for international road haulage have been abolished. EU shipowners are entitled to operate on all international routes within the Union. A single market has been established in civil aviation. Airlines of member states meeting established criteria, such as safety and financial fitness, are entitled to an operating licence allowing virtually unrestricted access to routes within the Union. They are free to set fares and rates according to commercial judgement.

In 1993 a regulation came into effect regarding the allocation of take-off and landing slots at airports in order to back up the single market in aviation; it aims to protect the legitimate interests of established carriers while promoting competition by assisting new entrants.

With the opening of the Channel Tunnel in 1994, there is a permanent rail link between Great Britain and continental Europe, allowing rail services to compete for international freight and passenger services.

Britain supports a number of initiatives designed to improve maritime safety and reduce the threat of pollution by shipping.

European Economic Area

The European Economic Area (EEA) Agreement entered into force on 1 January 1994. It extends most of the single market measures to Austria, Finland, Iceland, Norway and Sweden. It is hoped that Liechtenstein will join the EEA in the near future.

Trade

Britain is the world's fifth largest trading nation. EEA member states comprise the world's largest trading bloc, accounting for about a third of all trade.

The British Government fully supports an open world trading system, on which EU member states depend for future economic growth and jobs.

Under the Rome Treaty, the European Commission speaks on behalf of Britain and the other EU member states in international trade negotiations, such as the recently concluded GATT Uruguay Round. The Commission negotiates on a mandate agreed by the Council.

The Environment

European Union member states are at the forefront of many international measures on environmental issues, such as car exhaust pollution and the depletion of the ozone layer.

Agriculture and Fisheries

The Common Agriculture Policy (CAP) is designed to secure food supplies and to stabilise markets. It has also, however, created overproduction and unwanted food surpluses, placing a burden on the Community's budget.

The Common Fisheries Policy is concerned with the rational conservation and management of fishery resources.

Regional and Infrastructure Development

These are a number of Structural Funds designed to:

- promote economic development in poorer regions;
- improve regions seriously affected by industrial decline;
- combat long-term unemployment;
- train young people to find jobs:and
- promote development in rural areas.

Infrastructure projects and productive investments are financed by the European Regional Development Fund. The European Social Fund supports training and employment measures for the long-term unemployed and young people. The Guidance Section of the European Agricultural Guidance and Guarantee Fund supports agriculture restructuring and some rural development measures. A new fund to support restructuring in the fishing industry was created in 1993.

A new cohesion fund has been set up under the Maastricht Treaty to reduce disparities between levels of development in the poorer and richer member states.

Other programmes aim to assist the development of new economic activities in regions affected by the restructuring of traditional industries such as steel, coal and shipbuilding.

The European Investment Bank, a non-profit-making institution, lends at competitive interest rates to public and private capital projects. Lending is directed towards:

- less-favoured regions;
- transport infrastructure;
- protection of the environment;
- improving industrial competitiveness; and
- supporting loans to small and medium-sized enterprises.

The Bank also provides loans in support of the Community's policy of co-operation with the countries of the Mediterranean basin; Central and Eastern Europe; and the African, Caribbean and Pacific (ACP) states.

Employment and Social Affairs

In Britain's view, EC social policy should be primarily concerned with job creation and with maintaining a well-educated and trained workforce to ensure competitiveness in world markets. The Government supports:

- measures to safeguard health and safety at work, freedom of movement for workers, Union-wide recognition of professional and vocational qualifications, equal opportunities at work; and

- practical measures to increase jobs and cut unemployment which do not place more costs on employers.

At Maastricht the Government opposed the extension of Community social policy and qualified majority voting into new areas of social affairs on the grounds that the main responsibility for such policies should remain with individual member states. It negotiated the Social Protocol to the Maastricht Treaty, which allows other member states to agree social legislation in these areas which is not applicable in Britain.

Research and Development

Research collaboration among EU member states is promoted primarily through a series of framework programmes defining priorities and setting out the overall level of funding. The Fourth Framework Programme was adopted in April 1994. The British Government actively encourages British companies and organisations to participate in collaborative research and development (R & D) with European partners.

The Fourth Framework Programme gives priority to information and communications technology, industrial materials and technologies, the environment, biotechnology, agriculture, health and energy. There are also schemes for the exchange of researchers and for scientific collaboration with developing countries and the states of the former Soviet Union.

7.1   European Community regions

NETHERLANDS

1 Zuid-Nederland

BELGIUM

2 Vlaams Gewest
3 Région Wallone
4 Bruxelloise/Brussels

5 **LUXEMBOURG**

From: Regional Trends 1996

7.2 European Communities population and vital statistics

	Area (sq km) 1993	Population (thousands) 1993	Persons per sq km 1993	Percentage of population Aged under 15 1993	Aged 65 or over 1993	Births (per 1,000 population) 1993	Deaths (per 1,000 population) 1993	Infant mortality (per 1,000 births) 1992
EUR 15	3,191,120	369,794.9	115.9	17.9	15.0	11.2	10.1	6.9
Austria	83,859	7,991.5	95.3	17.6	14.9	11.9	10.3	7.5
Ostosterreich	23,554	3,367.6	143.0	16.0	16.5	11.1	11.9	8.0
Sudosterreich	25,921	1,760.9	67.9	17.8	15.2	11.2	10.2	6.7
Westosterreich	34,384	2,863.1	83.3	19.2	12.9	13.3	8.6	7.5
Belgium	30,518	10,084.5	330.4	18.2	15.8	11.9	10.6	6.9
Vlaams Gewest	13,512	5,835.8	431.9	17.9	15.3	11.6	10.0	6.7
Region Wallonne	16,844	3,298.9	195.8	18.8	16.0	11.9	11.4	7.3
Bruxelles-Brussels	161	949.7	5,884.2	17.5	17.9	13.1	11.5	7.0
Denmark	43,080	5,188.6	120.4	17.0	15.5	13.0	12.1	6.6
Finland	338,147	5,066.5	15.0	19.2	13.8	12.8	10.1	5.5
Manner-Suomi	336,595	5,041.4	15.0	19.2	13.7	12.8	10.1	5.5
Ahvenanmaa/Aland	1,552	25.0	16.1	18.4	16.4	13.1	9.9	-
France[1]	543,965	57,654.0	106.0	19.9	14.5	12.3	9.2	6.8
Ile de France	12,012	10,915.0	908.7	20.2	11.1	14.6	7.3	7.1
Bassin Parisien	145,645	10,419.9	71.5	20.7	14.7	12.1	9.5	7.2
Nord-Pas-de-Calais	12,414	3,998.3	322.1	23.3	12.5	13.6	9.2	7.1
Est	48,030	5,073.1	105.6	20.6	13.2	12.5	8.9	6.8
Ouest	85,099	7,579.1	89.1	19.9	15.9	11.2	9.7	6.3
Sud-Ouest	103,599	6,043.9	58.3	17.2	18.3	10.1	10.8	6.6
Centre-Est	69,711	6,811.0	97.7	19.9	14.3	12.2	8.9	6.1
Mediterranee	67,455	6,813.7	101.0	18.3	17.5	11.5	10.3	6.3
Germany[2]	356,718	81,172.2	227.6	16.4	15.0	9.8	11.1	6.2
Baden-Wuerttemberg	35,751	10,195.9	285.2	16.6	14.3	11.6	9.7	5.1
Bayern	70,554	11,816.8	167.5	16.2	15.1	11.3	10.4	5.3
Berlin	889	3,470.6	3,903.4	15.7	13.8	8.3	11.9	6.3
Brandenburg	29,480	2,546.0	86.4	19.4	12.5	4.8	11.4	7.5
Bremen	404	684.1	1,692.4	13.5	17.4	9.7	12.6	4.7
Hamburg	755	1,699.5	2,250.1	13.1	17.1	9.6	12.2	6.5
Hessen	21,114	5,945.0	281.6	15.1	15.4	10.4	10.8	5.8
Mecklenburg-Vorpommern	23,171	1,852.1	79.9	20.7	11.3	5.1	10.6	7.8
Niedersachsen	47,348	7,616.4	160.9	15.9	15.8	11.1	11.2	6.1
Nordrhein-Westfalen	34,072	17,721.6	520.1	15.9	15.3	11.0	11.0	7.0
Rheinland-Pfalz	19,846	3,903.4	196.7	16.2	16.0	10.8	11.2	6.7
Saarland	2,570	1,084.6	422.0	15.1	16.0	9.8	12.0	7.7
Sachsen	18,412	4,623.6	251.1	17.6	16.1	5.1	13.0	6.6
Sachsen-Anhalt	20,446	2,788.3	136.4	18.1	14.5	5.2	12.5	7.9
Schleswig-Holstein	15,732	2,686.7	170.8	15.2	15.9	10.7	11.6	5.7
Thueringen	16,174	2,537.6	156.9	18.6	14.1	5.2	11.8	7.8
Greece	131,625	10,380.4	78.9	18.1	14.6	9.8	9.4	8.4
Voreia Ellade	56,457	3,346.5	59.3	18.3	13.6	10.0	9.2	8.0
Kentriki Ellade	53,902	2,535.6	47.0	18.2	16.7	8.6	9.8	7.9
Attiki	3,808	3,500.7	919.3	17.4	13.7	10.3	9.1	9.6
Nisia Aigaiou, Kriti	17,458	997.6	57.1	19.6	16.4	10.7	10.1	6.5
Ireland	68,895	3,563.3	51.7	25.9	11.4	13.9	8.9	6.7

(continued overleaf)

7.2 continued

	Area (sq km) 1993	Popu-lation (thousands) 1993	Persons per sq km 1993	Percentage of population		Births (per 1,000 population) 1993	Deaths (per 1,000 population) 1993	Infant mortality (per 1,000 births) 1992
				Aged under 15 1993	Aged 65 or over 1993			
Italy	**301,316**	**57,138.5**	**189.6**	**15.5**	**15.7**	**9.7**	**9.7**	**8.0**
Nord Ovest	34,081	6,087.5	178.6	11.8	19.0	7.4	12.0	9.0
Lombardia	23,872	8,901.0	372.9	13.5	15.0	8.6	9.5	6.3
Nord Est	39,816	6,512.1	163.6	13.7	16.4	8.6	9.9	5.6
Emilia-Romagna	22,124	3,924.3	177.4	11.2	20.1	7.0	11.3	6.6
Centro	41,142	5,785.6	140.6	12.6	19.7	7.6	11.1	7.6
Lazio	17,227	5,185.3	301.0	15.0	14.6	9.6	9.2	9.7
Campania	15,232	1,594.9	104.7	16.2	17.5	9.7	10.2	8.8
Abruzzo-Molise	13,595	5,708.7	419.9	21.1	11.4	13.6	7.9	9.6
Sud	44,430	6,756.4	152.1	19.8	13.2	11.9	8.0	7.7
Sicilia	25,707	5,025.3	195.5	19.8	14.0	12.9	9.5	9.8
Sardegna	24,090	1,657.4	68.8	17.7	12.8	9.3	8.3	6.3
Luxembourg	**2,586**	**398.1**	**153.9**	**17.9**	**13.6**	**13.4**	**9.8**	**8.6**
Netherlands[3]	**41,029**	**15,288.8**	**372.6**	**18.3**	**13.0**	**12.8**	**9.0**	**6.3**
Noord-Nederland	11,388	1,611.3	141.5	18.2	14.2	12.0	9.8	6.5
Oost-Nederland	10,495	3,136.1	298.8	19.4	12.6	13.3	8.9	6.3
West-Nederland	11,854	7,167.2	604.6	18.0	13.5	13.0	9.3	6.3
Zuid-Nederland	7,292	3,374.2	462.7	18.1	11.9	12.3	8.2	6.2
Portugal	**91,906**	**9,876.1**	**107.5**	**18.9**	**14.0**	**11.5**	**10.8**	**9.3**
Continente	88,798	9,383.0	105.7	18.6	14.1	11.4	10.7	8.9
Acores	2,330	238.6	102.4	25.4	12.4	15.5	12.2	16.3
Maderia	779	254.6	326.8	23.0	11.8	13.7	10.8	11.2
Spain[4]	**504,790**	**39,082.6**	**77.4**	**18.0**	**14.2**	**9.9**	**8.7**	**7.4**
Noroeste	45,297	4,339.2	95.8	15.4	16.2	7.5	10.1	7.2
Noreste	70,366	4,056.7	57.7	15.3	15.0	8.1	8.9	8.0
Madrid	7,995	5,011.5	626.8	18.1	13.0	9.9	7.2	8.5
Centro	215,025	5,229.4	24.3	16.5	16.6	9.3	9.6	5.5
Este	60,249	10,709.5	177.8	17.6	14.7	9.7	8.9	6.6
Sur	98,616	8,212.8	83.3	21.4	12.1	12.3	8.0	8.8
Canarias	7,242	1,523.6	210.4	20.9	9.9	11.3	6.9	5.2
Sweden	**410,934**	**8,718.6**	**21.2**	**18.5**	**18.2**	**13.5**	**11.1**	**5.5**
United Kingdom	**241,752**	**58,191.2**	**240.7**	**19.4**	**15.8**	**13.1**	**11.3**	**6.6**
North	15,415	3,102.3	201.2	19.4	16.0	12.4	12.2	7.1
Yorkshire & Humberside	15,411	5,014.1	325.4	19.4	15.9	13.0	11.4	6.7
East Midlands	15,627	4,082.9	261.3	19.3	15.8	12.7	11.1	6.9
East Anglia	12,570	2,093.9	166.6	18.7	17.1	12.2	11.1	4.6
South East	27,224	17,769.4	652.7	19.0	15.1	13.7	10.4	6.1
South West	23,829	4,768.0	200.1	18.1	18.6	11.9	11.9	5.7
West Midlands	13,004	5,289.6	406.8	19.8	15.4	13.2	11.0	8.2
North West	7,342	6,412.4	873.4	20.1	15.6	13.2	12.1	7.0
Wales	20,766	2,906.5	140.0	19.5	17.3	12.6	12.3	5.9
Scotland	77,080	5,120.2	66.4	19.0	15.1	12.4	12.5	6.8
Northern Ireland	13,483	1,631.8	121.0	24.2	12.7	15.3	9.6	6.0

1 The regional data for France are estimates.
2 All data refer to the unified German state. Data for Berlin refer to the 'New' Berlin (East + West).
3 Including 'centraal persoons register'.
4 The regional birth and death rates are estimates.

Source: Statistical Office of the European Communities

From: Regional Trends 1996, Table 2.1

7.3 UK nationals living in other EC states[1] and nationals of other EC states living in the UK[1], 1994

Thousands

	UK nationals living in other EC states	EC nationals living in the United Kingdom
Irish Republic	56	482
Italy	21	79
Germany	111	47
France	50	57
Spain	58	41
Greece	14	19
Netherlands	45	29
Portugal	11	30
Sweden	11	13
Denmark	11	11
Finland	2	6
Austria	3	6
Belgium	25	7
All	421	827

1 Data are not available for Luxembourg.

Source: Eurostat

From: Social Trends 1996, Table 1.18

7.4 Marriage and divorce rates: EC comparison, 1981 and 1994

Rates per 1,000 population

	Marriages		Divorces	
	1981	1994	1981	1994
United Kingdom	7.1	5.9[1]	2.8	3.1[1]
Denmark	5.0	6.8	2.8	2.6
Finland	6.3	4.9	2.0	2.7
Sweden	4.5	3.9	2.4	2.5
Belgium	6.5	5.1	1.6	2.2
Austria	6.3	5.4	1.8	2.1
Netherlands	6.0	5.4	2.0	2.4
France	5.8	4.4	1.6	1.9[1]
Germany	6.2	5.4	2.0	2.0
Luxembourg	5.5	5.8	1.4	1.7
Portugal	7.8	6.7	0.7	1.4
Greece	6.9	5.4	0.7	0.7
Spain	5.4	5.0	0.3	0.7[1]
Italy	5.6	5.0	0.2	0.5
Irish Republic	6.0	4.6	.	.
EC average	6.1	5.2	1.5	1.7[1]

1 1993 figure; 1994 data not yet available.

Source: Eurostat

From: Social Trends 1996, Table 2.16

7.5 Death rates[1] for selected diseases: EC comparison, 1992

Rates per 100,000 population

	Malignant neoplasms		Diseases of the circulatory system		Cerebrovascular disease	
	Males	Females	Males	Females	Males	Females
Austria	257	157	473	316	102	80
Belgium[2]	312	160	379	239	80	66
Denmark	272	204	443	263	81	65
Finland	232	135	535	289	104	83
France	295	129	255	151	61	44
Germany	273	162	473	300	99	79
Greece	218	113	395	300	125	126
Irish Republic	271	187	504	302	85	78
Italy[3]	284	146	376	248	105	81
Luxembourg	303	160	413	272	112	102
Netherlands	295	160	370	214	74	63
Portugal	222	126	447	317	231	176
Spain[3]	255	119	335	242	97	82
Sweden	197	143	421	244	74	61
United Kingdom	275	182	450	266	91	80
EC average	273	151	395	251	94	77

1 Age standardised.
2 Data are for 1989.
3 Data are for 1991.

Source: World Health Organisation

From: Social Trends 1996, Table 7.23

7.6 People in full-time and part-time employment: EC comparison, 1994

Percentages

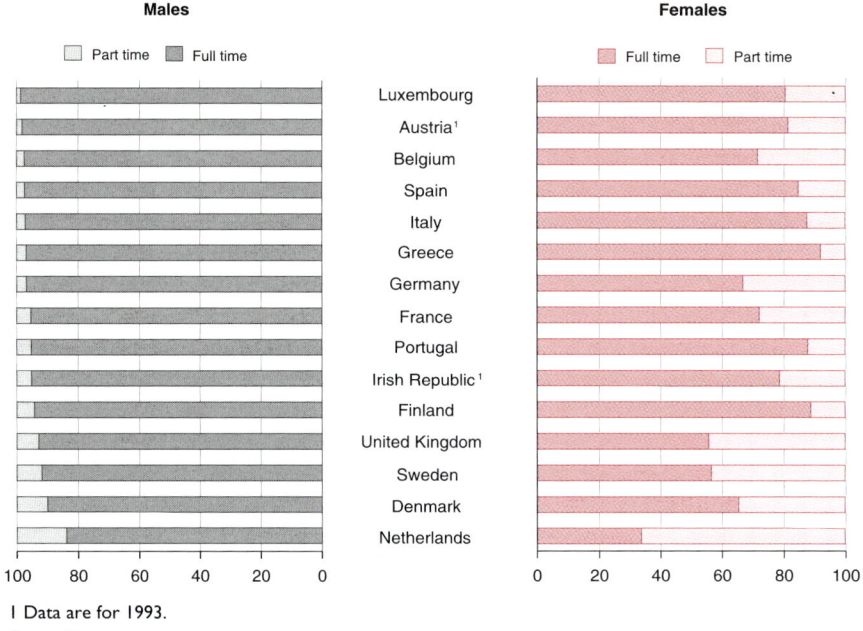

I Data are for 1993.

Source: Eurostat

From: Social Trends 1996, Chart 4.8

7.7 Passenger traffic: by mode, EC comparison, 1993

Thousand kilometres per head

	Cars and taxis	Buses and coaches	Rail[1]	All these modes[1]
Austria	8.4	1.7	1.2	11.4
Belgium	8.6	0.5	0.7	9.8
Denmark	10.9	1.8	0.9	13.5
Finland	9.8	1.6	0.6	12.0
France	11.0	0.7	1.0	12.7
Germany	8.8	0.9	0.7	10.3
Great Britain	9.6	0.7	0.5	10.9
Greece	..	0.5	0.2	..
Irish Republic	..	..	0.4	..
Italy	10.6	1.5	0.8	12.9
Luxembourg	..	..	0.7	..
Netherlands	9.2	0.8	1.0	11.0
Portugal	7.7	1.2	0.5	9.4
Spain	5.3	0.8	0.4	6.5
Sweden	10.4	1.2	0.7	12.3

I Excluding metro systems.

Source: Department of Transport

From: Social Trends 1996, Table 12.2

eight

Prices & expenditure

Definitions and sources

The Retail Prices Index (RPI) measures the changes month by month in the level of prices of the goods and services purchased by all types of household in the UK, with the exception of some higher income households and retired people mainly dependent on state benefits. A special pensioner price index is published in the *Business Monitor MM23* and *Economic Trends*.

The Tax and Price Index (TPI) is described in a footnote to the table in which it appears.

The Producer Price Index (MM22) has replaced what was called the Wholesale Price Index. The new title is more accurate and conforms with international nomenclatures. The index was also re-based from 1985 to 1990. Full details were given in an article in *British Business*, 15 April 1983.

For other sources see: *Guide to Official Statistics, 1996 edition* (520 pages approximately, fully indexed) HMSO.

8.1 Retail Prices Index

13 January 1987=100

| | | All items excluding | | | | | | | | | | All items excluding |
	ALL ITEMS (RPI)	Mortgage interest payments (RPIX)	Mortgage interest payments and deprec-ation[1]	Hous-ing	Food	Seas-onal food[2]	Food and cater-ing	Alcohol and tobacco	Housing and house-hold expen-diture	Pers-onal expen-diture	Travel and leisure	Consumer durables	mortgage interest payments & indirect taxes (RPIY)[3]
Weights													
1987	1 000	956	956	843	833	974	213	114	335	112	226	139	
1988	1 000	958	958	840	837	975	213	114	330	109	234	141	
1989	1 000	940	940	825	846	977	203	119	341	110	227	135	
1990	1 000	925	925	815	842	976	205	111	346	108	230	132	
1991	1 000	924	924	808	849	976	198	109	353	101	239	128	
1992	1 000	936	936	828	848	978	199	116	344	99	242	127	
1993	1 000	952	952	836	856	979	189	113	336	97	265	127	
1994	1 000	956	956	842	858	980	187	111	326	95	281	127	
1995	1 000	958	928	813	861	978	184	111	356	93	256	123	
1996	1 000	958	929	810	857	978	191	113	353	92	251	116	

(continued overleaf)

8.1 Retail Prices Index
continued

13 January 1987=100

	ALL ITEMS (RPI)	Mortgage interest payments (RPIX)	All items excluding					Alcohol and tobacco	Housing and house-hold expen-diture	Pers-onal expen-diture	Travel and leisure	Consumer durables	All items excluding mortgage interest payments & indirect taxes (RPIY)[3]
			Mortgage interest payments and deprec-ation[1]	Hous-ing	Food	Seas-onal food[2]	Food and cater-ing						

Annual averages

	ALL ITEMS (RPI)	(RPIX)	deprec-ation[1]	Hous-ing	Food	Seasonal food[2]	Food and catering	Alcohol and tobacco	Housing and household	Personal	Travel and leisure	Consumer durables	(RPIY)[3]
1987	101.9	101.9	101.9	101.6	102.0	101.9	101.4	101.2	102.1	101.4	102.6	101.2	101.9
1988	106.9	106.6	106.6	105.8	107.3	107.0	105.7	105.7	108.4	105.2	107.2	103.7	106.6
1989	115.2	112.9	112.9	111.5	116.1	115.5	111.9	110.8	121.9	111.3	112.8	107.2	113.1
1990	126.1	122.1	122.1	119.2	127.4	126.4	120.9	120.6	139.0	117.6	119.8	111.3	121.4
1991	133.5	130.3	130.3	128.3	135.1	133.8	128.6	136.2	142.2	123.6	128.9	114.8	129.5
1992	138.5	136.4	136.4	134.3	140.5	139.1	132.6	146.8	144.2	126.9	136.8	115.5	135.1
1993	140.7	140.5	140.5	138.4	142.6	141.4	136.1	155.1	141.2	129.5	141.8	115.9	139.0
1994	144.1	143.8	143.8	141.6	146.5	144.8	138.5	161.4	144.4	131.9	145.7	115.5	141.3
1995	149.1	147.9	148.0	145.4	151.4	149.6	143.9	169.0	150.8	133.6	148.4	116.2	144.5

Monthly figures

	ALL ITEMS (RPI)	(RPIX)	deprec-ation[1]	Hous-ing	Food	Seasonal food[2]	Food and catering	Alcohol and tobacco	Housing and household	Personal	Travel and leisure	Consumer durables	(RPIY)[3]
1993 Apr	140.6	140.6	140.6	138.4	142.5	141.3	136.0	154.7	141.1	130.1	141.6	117.0	139.0
May	141.1	141.0	141.0	139.0	142.8	141.6	137.2	155.3	141.0	130.5	142.1	117.3	139.6
Jun	141.0	141.0	141.0	138.9	142.9	141.7	136.8	155.5	140.7	129.6	143.0	116.3	139.5
Jul	140.7	140.6	140.6	138.5	142.6	141.5	136.8	156.0	140.5	127.0	142.9	113.3	139.1
Aug	141.3	141.2	141.2	139.1	143.2	142.1	137.0	156.8	141.1	128.5	143.3	114.8	139.7
Sep	141.9	141.8	141.8	139.8	144.1	142.8	136.7	157.4	141.5	131.5	143.9	117.0	140.4
Oct	141.8	141.7	141.7	139.6	144.1	142.7	136.1	157.7	141.6	131.9	143.6	116.9	140.2
Nov	141.6	141.4	141.4	139.3	144.0	142.5	135.5	157.2	141.9	132.4	142.8	117.4	139.9
Dec	141.9	141.8	141.8	139.7	144.3	142.8	135.8	157.8	142.0	132.0	143.6	117.6	139.6
1994 Jan	141.3	141.3	141.3	139.3	143.5	142.1	136.3	159.8	140.3	127.8	144.0	113.0	139.2
Feb	142.1	142.2	142.2	140.2	144.3	142.9	137.0	160.3	140.6	131.0	144.6	114.8	140.1
Mar	142.5	142.6	142.6	140.6	144.7	143.2	137.8	160.2	140.9	131.5	145.1	116.2	140.5
Apr	144.2	143.9	143.9	141.6	146.5	144.9	138.2	160.7	144.8	131.9	145.7	116.0	141.3
May	144.7	144.5	144.5	142.1	146.9	145.2	139.3	161.0	145.0	132.9	146.1	116.2	141.9
Jun	144.7	144.4	144.4	142.1	147.0	145.3	139.3	161.5	145.1	132.1	146.2	115.9	141.9
Jul	144.0	143.7	143.7	141.2	146.2	144.6	138.8	162.0	144.6	128.6	145.6	112.3	141.1
Aug	144.7	144.4	144.4	142.0	147.0	145.3	139.3	162.1	145.3	131.2	146.1	114.4	141.7
Sep	145.0	144.7	144.7	142.3	147.6	145.7	138.5	162.4	145.6	133.7	146.3	116.3	142.2
Oct	145.2	144.5	144.5	142.1	147.8	145.9	138.5	162.4	146.5	133.3	146.0	116.1	141.9
Nov	145.3	144.6	144.6	142.2	147.9	146.0	139.0	162.0	146.9	133.8	145.7	116.9	141.9
Dec	146.0	145.3	145.3	142.9	148.5	146.6	139.7	162.5	147.3	134.6	146.5	117.4	142.1
1995 Jan	146.0	145.2	145.2	142.9	148.3	146.5	141.0	165.6	146.8	130.2	146.9	113.2	141.8
Feb	146.9	146.0	146.0	143.7	149.2	147.3	141.8	166.9	148.0	131.1	147.3	114.8	142.6
Mar	147.5	146.6	146.7	144.5	149.8	148.0	142.7	167.5	148.4	132.5	147.8	116.2	143.2
Apr	149.0	147.7	147.8	145.0	151.5	149.4	142.7	168.0	151.6	133.9	148.2	116.5	144.2
May	149.6	148.4	148.6	145.8	151.8	150.0	144.7	168.9	151.7	134.5	148.4	117.2	145.0
Jun	149.8	148.5	148.6	145.8	152.2	150.4	143.9	169.5	152.1	134.2	149.0	116.9	145.1
Jul	149.1	147.7	147.9	145.0	151.6	149.9	143.2	170.1	151.3	130.8	149.1	113.4	144.3
Aug	149.9	148.6	148.7	145.9	152.1	150.3	145.5	170.0	151.9	132.2	149.2	114.9	145.2
Sep	150.6	149.2	149.4	146.7	152.8	151.0	145.9	170.3	152.4	135.5	149.3	117.5	145.9
Oct	149.8	148.7	148.9	146.2	152.1	150.5	144.8	170.8	151.4	135.5	148.4	117.2	145.3
Nov	149.8	148.8	148.9	146.2	152.2	150.5	145.0	170.2	151.8	136.1	147.9	118.1	145.3
Dec	150.7	149.6	149.8	147.2	152.9	151.3	146.0	170.5	152.1	136.3	149.6	119.0	145.6
1996 Jan	150.2	149.3	149.5	146.8	152.3	150.7	146.7	172.6	150.9	131.4	150.2	113.8	145.3
Feb	150.9	150.2	150.2	147.6	152.8	151.3	148.0	173.6	151.4	132.7	150.3	115.5	146.2
Mar	151.5	150.9	150.9	148.4	153.3	151.9	149.0	173.9	151.9	134.1	150.6	117.4	146.9
Apr	152.6	152.0	152.1	149.0	154.6	153.0	149.2	174.8	153.3	135.4	151.8	117.5	147.9

1 This series has been constructed using the index for all items excluding mortgage interest payments prior to February 1995.
2 Seasonal food is defined as items of food the prices of which show significant seasonal variations. These are fresh fruit and vegetables, fresh fish, eggs and home-killed lamb.
3 There are no weights available for RPIY.

Source: Office for National Statistics

From: Monthly Digest of Statistics, May 1996, Table 18.1

8.2 Tax and Price Index

Tax and Price Index: January 1987 = 100									
	1987	1988	1989	1990	1991	1992	1993	1994	1995	1996
January	100.0	101.4	107.1	113.9	123.6	128.1	128.7	132.1	137.2	141.6
February	100.5	101.8	108.0	114.7	124.3	128.8	129.6	132.9	138.2	142.3
March	100.7	102.3	108.5	115.9	124.9	129.3	130.2	133.4	138.8	143.0
April	99.7	101.4	109.8	118.2	125.4	129.6	131.3	135.3	140.3	141.7
May	99.8	101.9	110.5	119.4	125.8	130.2	131.8	135.8	141.0	..
June	99.8	102.3	110.9	119.9	126.5	130.2	131.7	135.8	141.2	..
July	99.7	102.4	111.1	120.0	126.2	129.6	131.4	135.1	140.4	..
August	100.0	103.7	111.4	121.4	126.5	129.7	132.1	135.8	141.3	..
September	100.4	104.3	112.2	122.7	127.0	130.3	132.7	136.1	142.0	..
October	100.9	105.4	111.7	123.8	127.5	130.8	132.6	136.4	141.2	..
November	101.5	106.0	112.8	123.4	128.1	130.6	132.4	136.5	141.2	..
December	101.4	106.3	113.1	123.3	128.2	130.1	132.7	137.2	142.1	..

Retail Prices Index: January 1987 = 100									
	1987	1988	1989	1990	1991	1992	1993	1994	1995	1996
January	100.0	103.3	111.0	119.5	130.2	135.6	137.9	141.3	146.0	150.2
February	100.4	103.7	111.8	120.2	130.9	136.3	138.8	142.1	146.9	150.9
March	100.6	104.1	112.3	121.4	131.4	136.7	139.3	142.5	147.5	151.5
April	101.8	105.8	114.3	125.1	133.1	138.8	140.6	144.2	149.0	152.6
May	101.9	106.2	115.0	126.2	133.5	139.3	141.1	144.7	149.6	..
June	101.9	106.6	115.4	126.7	134.1	139.3	141.0	144.7	149.8	..
July	101.8	106.7	115.5	126.8	133.8	138.8	140.7	144.0	149.1	..
August	102.1	107.9	115.8	128.1	134.1	138.9	141.3	144.7	149.9	..
September	102.4	108.4	116.6	129.3	134.6	139.4	141.9	145.0	150.6	..
October	102.9	109.5	117.5	130.3	135.1	139.9	141.8	145.2	149.8	..
November	103.4	110.0	118.5	130.0	135.6	139.7	141.6	145.3	149.8	..
December	103.3	110.3	118.8	129.9	135.7	139.2	141.9	146.0	150.7	..

Percentage changes on one year earlier									
	1988	1989	1990	1991	1992	1993	1994	1995	1996

Tax and Price Index

	1988	1989	1990	1991	1992	1993	1994	1995	1996
January	1.4	5.6	6.3	8.5	3.6	0.5	2.6	3.9	3.2
February	1.3	6.1	6.2	8.4	3.6	0.6	2.5	4.0	3.0
March	1.6	6.1	6.8	7.8	3.5	0.7	2.5	4.0	3.0
April	1.7	8.3	7.7	6.1	3.3	1.3	3.0	3.7	1.0
May	2.1	8.4	8.1	5.4	3.5	1.2	3.0	3.8	..
June	2.5	8.4	8.1	5.5	2.9	1.2	3.1	4.0	..
July	2.7	8.5	8.0	5.2	2.7	1.4	2.8	3.9	..
August	3.7	7.4	9.0	4.2	2.5	1.9	2.8	4.1	..
September	3.9	7.6	9.4	3.5	2.6	1.8	2.6	4.3	..
October	4.5	6.0	10.8	3.0	2.6	1.4	2.9	3.5	..
November	4.4	6.4	9.4	3.8	2.0	1.4	3.1	3.4	..
December	4.8	6.4	9.0	4.0	1.5	2.0	3.4	3.6	..

Retail Prices Index

	1988	1989	1990	1991	1992	1993	1994	1995	1996
January	3.3	7.5	7.7	9.0	4.1	1.7	2.5	3.3	2.9
February	3.3	7.8	7.5	8.9	4.1	1.8	2.4	3.4	2.7
March	3.5	7.9	8.1	8.2	4.0	1.9	2.3	3.5	2.7
April	3.9	8.0	9.4	6.4	4.3	1.3	2.8	3.3	2.4
May	4.2	8.3	9.7	5.8	4.3	1.3	2.6	3.4	..
June	4.6	8.3	9.8	5.8	3.9	1.2	2.6	3.5	..
July	4.8	8.2	9.8	5.5	3.7	1.4	2.3	3.5	..
August	5.7	7.3	10.6	4.7	3.6	1.7	2.4	3.6	..
September	5.9	7.6	10.9	4.1	3.6	1.8	2.2	3.9	..
October	6.4	7.3	10.9	3.7	3.6	1.4	2.4	3.2	..
November	6.4	7.7	9.7	4.3	3.0	1.4	2.6	3.1	..
December	6.8	7.7	9.3	4.5	2.6	1.9	2.9	3.2	..

Note: The purpose and methodology of the Tax and Price Index were described in an article in the August 1979 issue of *Economic trends*. The purpose is to produce a single index which measures changes in both direct taxes (including national insurance contributions) and in retail prices for a representative cross-section of taxpayers. Thus, while the Retail Prices Index may be used to measure changes in the purchasing power of after-tax income (and of the income of non-taxpayers) the Tax and Price Index takes account of the fact that taxpayers will have more or less to spend according to changes in direct taxation. The index measures the change in gross taxable income which would maintain their after-tax income in real terms.

Source: Office for National Statistics

From: Monthly Digest of Statistics, May 1996, Table 18.5

8.3 Household expenditure on selected items

United Kingdom

Percentages

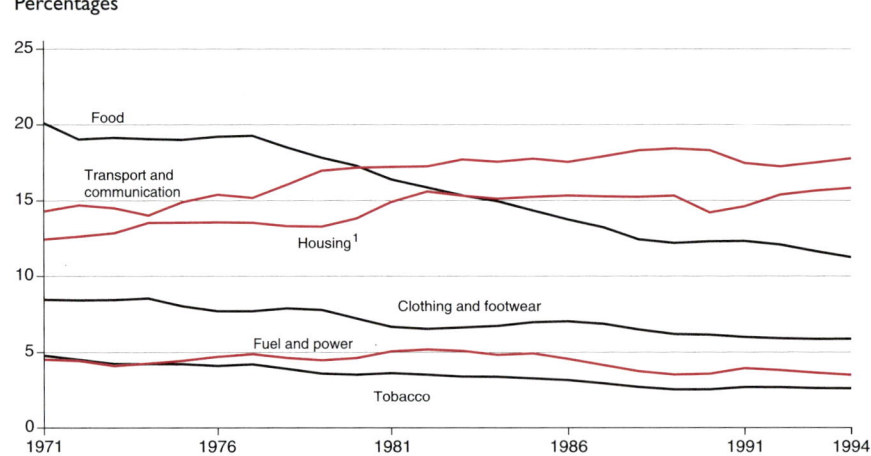

1 Includes domestic rates, but excludes community charge and council tax.

Source: Office for National Statistics

From: Social Trends 1996, Chart 6.1

8.4 Consumers' expenditure at 1990 market prices: classified by commodity[1]

£ million at 1990 prices

	1984	1985	1986	1987	1988	1989	1990	1991	1992	1993	1994
Durable goods:											
Cars, motorcycles and other vehicles	13 453	14 162	15 552	16 525	19 410	21 031	19 034	15 415	14 634	16 460	18 865
Furniture and floor coverings	5 039	5 145	5 573	6 043	6 858	6 748	6 422	6 070	6 137	6 680	7 148
Other durable goods	5 647	5 966	6 802	7 829	8 785	9 090	9 220	9 355	9 906	10 635	11 699
Total	24 059	25 192	27 927	30 397	35 053	36 869	34 676	30 840	30 677	33 775	37 712
Other goods:											
Food (household expenditure)	37 925	38 402	39 610	40 621	41 542	42 247	41 817	41 869	42 384	42 991	43 437
Beer	11 651	11 609	11 595	11 822	11 960	11 956	11 904	11 438	10 724	10 375	10 533
Other alcoholic drink	8 812	9 217	9 293	9 443	9 700	9 550	9 455	9 129	8 983	9 270	9 847
Tobacco	9 238	8 990	8 771	8 706	8 729	8 730	8 649	8 437	7 969	7 562	7 431
Clothing other than footwear	13 022	14 207	15 618	16 582	17 234	17 096	17 245	17 387	17 906	18 740	19 689
Footwear	3 250	3 415	3 551	3 622	3 546	3 566	3 631	3 430	3 549	3 729	4 018
Energy products	19 299	20 191	21 420	21 871	22 482	22 335	22 422	23 151	22 889	23 021	22 694
Other goods	27 387	28 712	31 035	33 490	36 308	38 486	39 566	38 550	38 740	40 179	41 380
Services:											
Rents, rates and water charges	35 932	36 401	36 896	37 407	37 959	38 428	38 916	39 324	39 647	39 999	40 370
Other services[2]	75 796	80 334	89 906	97 273	110 078	116 143	119 246	116 360	116 069	118 806	121 772
Total consumers' expenditure	266 486	276 742	295 622	311 234	334 591	345 406	347 527	339 915	339 537	348 447	358 883

1 For the years before 1986, totals differ from the sum of their components.
2 Including the adjustments for international travel, etc and final expenditure by private non-profit-making bodies serving persons.

Source: Office for National Statistics

From: Annual Abstract of Statistics 1996, Table 14.12.

8.5 Net lending to consumers[1]

United Kingdom

£ billion

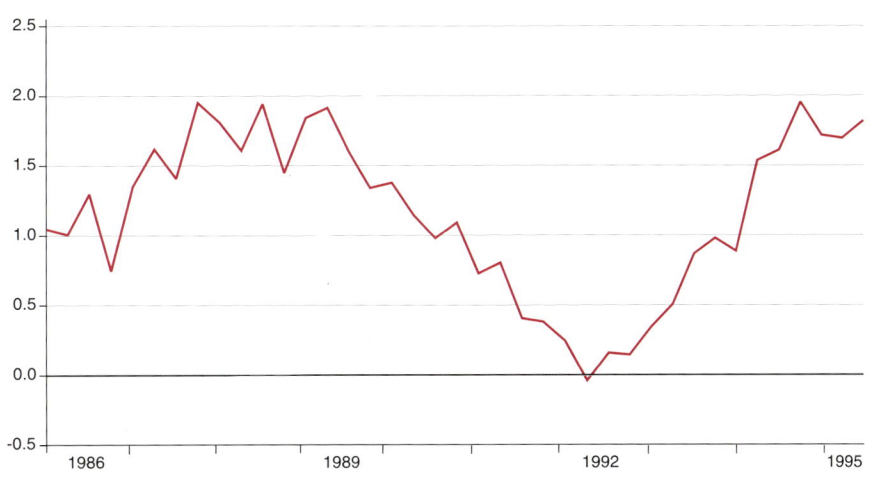

1 Seasonally adjusted.

Source: Office for National Statistics

From: Social Trends 1996, Chart 6.17

8.6 Composition of consumer credit

United Kingdom Percentages

	1987	1991	1992	1993	1994
Bank loans[1]	63	63	63	59	57
Bank credit card lending	16	18	18	20	20
Other specialist lenders[2]	12	11	10	13	14
Retailers	6	5	5	5	5
Insurance companies	3	2	2	3	2
Building Society loans[3]	-	1	1	1	2
Credit outstanding at end of year (=100%)(£ billion at 1994 prices[4])	51.8	58.8	55.7	54.6	58.3

1 Banks and all other institutions authorised to take deposits under the Banking Act 1987.
2 Finance houses and other credit companies (excluding institutions authorised to take deposits under the Banking Act 1987).
3 Building Society unsecured loans to individuals or companies (ie Class 3 loans as defined in the Building Societies Act 1986).
4 Adjusted to 1994 prices using the retail prices index.

Source: Office for National Statistics

From: Social Trends 1996, Table 6.16

8.7 **Household saving as a percentage of household disposable income**

United Kingdom

Percentages

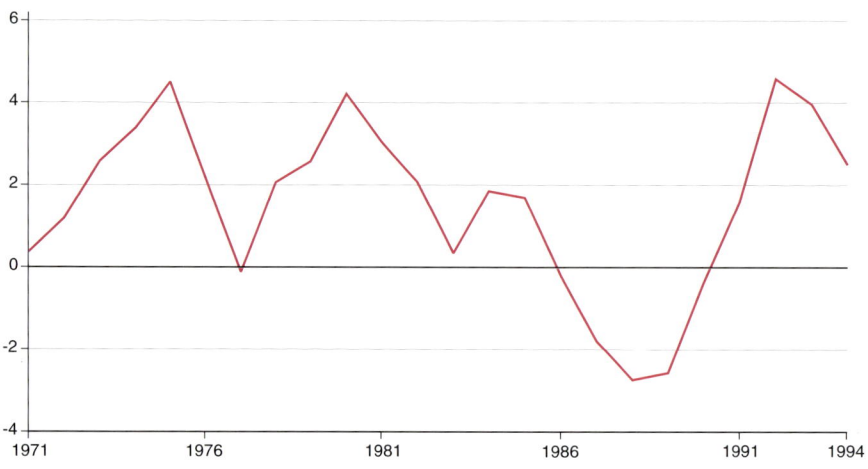

Source: Office for National Statistics

From: Social Trends 1996, Chart 6.20

8.8 **Type of savings[1]: by working status and gender, 1993[2]**

Great Britain   Percentages

| | Employed | | | | | | |
	Full time	Part time	Retired	Not working	Males	Females	All adults
Bank account	89	83	81	70	83	79	81
Building society account	69	71	68	55	64	66	65
Premium bonds	29	28	39	20	28	28	28
Company shares[3]	16	11	13	5	14	9	12
Government privatisation shares	12	8	14	6	13	8	10
National Savings Bank Investment/Ordinary account	10	12	10	9	10	10	10
Unit or investment trusts	10	8	12	5	11	7	9
National Savings certificates/ bonds	5	7	14	6	8	7	7
Personal equity plan	8	5	7	3	8	4	6

1 Held by adults.
2 Fieldwork took place in February and March 1993.
3 Excludes government privatisations.

Source: Building Societies Association

From: Social Trends 1996, Table 6.19

nine

Incomes

Definitions and sources

The household sector includes private trusts and individuals living in institutions as well as those living in households. It differs from the personal sector, as defined in the national accounts, in that it excludes unincorporated private businesses, private non-profit-making bodies serving persons, and funds of life assurance and pension schemes.

Household disposable income is equal to the total current income of the household sector *less* payment of United Kingdom taxes on income, employees' national insurance contributions, and contributions of employees to occupational pension schemes. It is revalued at constant prices by a deflator implied by estimates of total household expenditure at current and constant prices. This deflator is a modified form of the consumers' expenditure deflator.

Quintile group is the main method of analysing income distribution used in this chapter to rank units (households, individuals, etc) by a given income measure dividing the ranked units into groups of equal size. Groups comprising 20 per cent of units are known as 'quintile groups'. Thus the 'bottom quintile group' is the 20 per cent of units with the lowest incomes.

For other sources see: Guide to Official Statistics, 1996 edition (520 pages approximately, fully indexed) HMSO.
Inland Revenue Statistics, HMSO.
Family Spending, HMSO.

9.1 Household income[1]

United Kingdom — Percentages

	1971	1976	1981	1986	1991	1994
Source of income						
Wages and salaries[1]	68	67	63	58	58	57
Income from self-employment[2]	9	9	8	10	10	10
Rent, dividends, interest	6	6	7	8	9	6
Private pensions, annuities, etc	5	5	6	8	10	11
Social security benefits	10	11	13	13	11	13
Other current transfers[3]	2	2	2	3	2	3
Total household income (=100%)(£ billion at 1994 prices[4])	305	354	386	458	556	564
Direct taxes, etc as a percentage of total household income						
Taxes on income	14	17	14	14	14	13
National insurance contributions[5]	3	3	3	4	3	3
Contributions to pension schemes	1	2	2	2	2	2
Total household disposable income (£ billion at 1994 prices[4])	248	276	310	368	453	466

1 Includes Forces' pay and income in kind.
2 After deducting interest payments, depreciation and stock appreciation.
3 Mostly other government grants, but including transfers from abroad and non-profit making bodies.
4 Adjusted to 1994 prices using the consumers' expenditure deflator.
5 By employees and the self-employed.

Source: Office for National Statistics

From: Social Trends 1996, Table 5.2

9.2 Pensioners'[1] gross income: by source

United Kingdom   Percentages

	1981	1990-1991	1992	1993
Benefits	61	50	50	53
Occupational pensions	16	22	24	25
Investments	13	20	20	16
Earnings	9	7	6	6
Other	-	1	1	-
All gross income (=100%)				
(£ per week at July 1993 prices[2])	120.60	163.30	170.40	170.20

1 Pensioner units.
2 Adjusted to July 1993 prices using the retail prices index less local taxes.
Source: Department of Social Security

From: Social Trends 1996, Table 5.5

9.3 Average weekly and hourly earnings and hours of full-time employees on adult rates

Great Britain   At April

	All Industries				Manufacturing Industries			
			Average hourly earnings				Average hourly earnings	
	Average weekly earnings[1]	Average hours	including overtime	excluding overtime	Average weekly earnings	Average hours	including overtime	excluding overtime
	£		£	£	£		£	£
All adults								
1994	325.7	40.1	8.03	8.03	321.6	41.7	7.62	7.58
1995	336.3	40.3	8.31	8.32	334.3	42.2	7.92	7.85
All men								
1994	362.1	41.6	8.61	8.65	350.9	42.5	8.16	8.12
1995	374.6	41.9	8.91	8.97	364.0	43.0	8.44	8.41
Manual men								
1994	280.7	44.7	6.31	6.14	296.9	44.1	6.72	6.50
1995	291.3	45.2	6.44	6.25	313.4	44.9	6.98	6.74
Non-manual men								
1994	428.2	38.9	10.90	10.93	434.7	39.7	10.79	10.84
1995	443.3	39.0	11.33	11.36	449.2	39.9	11.24	11.29
All women								
1994	261.5	37.6	6.89	6.88	226.8	39.1	5.76	5.72
1995	269.8	37.6	7.15	7.14	236.7	39.4	6.01	5.96
Manual women								
1994	181.9	40.1	4.53	4.45	186.4	40.6	4.59	4.49
1995	188.1	40.2	4.64	4.55	198.5	40.9	4.86	4.74
Non-manual women								
1994	278.4	37.0	7.44	7.42	263.2	37.7	6.94	6.92
1995	288.1	37.0	7.76	7.75	275.0	37.8	7.26	7.23

1 Excluding those whose pay was affected by absence.
Source: New Earnings Survey; Office for National Statistics

From: Annual Abstract of Statistics 1996, Table 6.15.

9.4 Gross weekly earnings[1]: by gender and age, April 1995

United Kingdom

£ per week

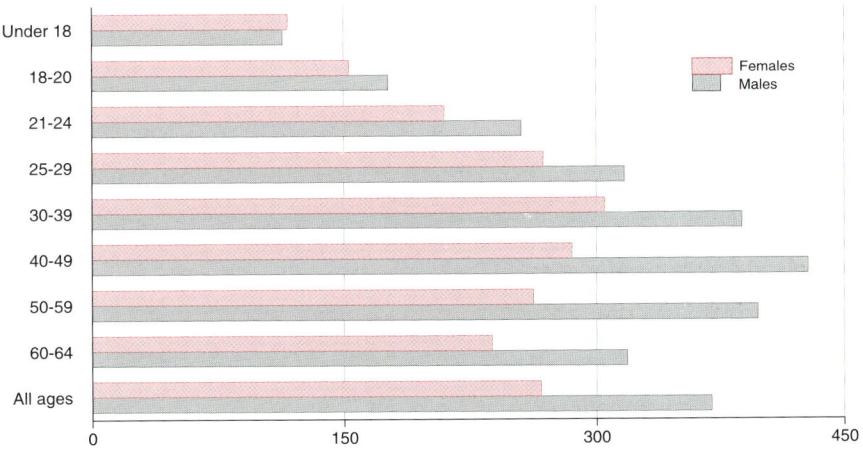

1 Full-time employees on all rates whose pay was not affected for the survey period by absence.

Source: New Earnings Survey, Office for National Statistics

From: Social Trends 1996, Chart 5.8

9.5 Real[1] gross weekly earnings[2]: by selected occupation

Great Britain				£ per week at April 1995 prices[1]		
	1971	1976	1981	1986	1991	1995
Waiter/waitress	108	155	143	156	166	161
Bar staff	119	148	148	165	158	165
Cleaner	113	180	175	185	186	181
Receptionist	117	132	139	158	179	188
Caretaker	163	197	185	203	220	227
Bricklayer/mason	204	252	232	242	256	263
Carpenter/joiner	209	244	230	244	269	274
Nurse	146	194	194	223	308	329
Social worker	209	236	254	273	313	340
Primary teacher	} 243 {	295	301	312	370	401
Secondary teacher		327	324	333	403	435
Mechanical engineer	332	377	387	437	510	503
Solicitor	359	392	379	432	610	585
Medical practitioner	515	504	569	612	691	764

1 Adjusted to April 1995 prices using the retail prices index.
2 At April each year. Full-time employees on adult rates whose pay was not affected for the survey period by absence.

Source: New Earnings Survey, Office for National Statistics

From: Social Trends 1996, Table 5.7

9.6 Redistribution of income through taxes and benefits, 1994-95

United Kingdom   £ per year

	Quintile groups of households[1]					All house-holds
	Bottom fifth	Next fifth	Middle fifth	Next fifth	Top fifth	
Average per household						
Wages and salaries	1,180	3,830	10,230	17,820	28,250	12,260
Imputed income from benefits in kind	10	20	100	310	950	280
Self-employment income	260	510	1,050	1,550	6,160	1,910
Occupational pensions, annuities	280	780	1,300	1,520	2,220	1,220
Investment income	170	260	500	800	2,420	830
Other income	140	200	190	250	340	230
Total original income	2,040	5,600	13,380	22,250	40,330	16,720
plus Benefits in cash						
Contributory	1,930	2,290	1,620	1,050	680	1,510
Non-contributory	2,730	2,180	1,540	900	490	1,570
Gross income	6,700	10,080	16,540	24,200	41,510	19,800
less Income tax[2] and NIC[3]	270	760	2,300	4,360	9,350	3,410
less Local taxes[4] (gross)	570	550	630	680	790	640
Disposable income	5,860	8,760	13,610	19,150	31,370	15,750
less Indirect taxes	1,740	2,070	3,090	3,960	4,810	3,130
Post-tax income	4,120	6,700	10,520	15,190	26,570	12,620
plus Benefits in kind						
Education	1,600	1,250	1,390	1,200	670	1,220
National Health Service	1,790	1,720	1,660	1,460	1,270	1,580
Housing subsidy	80	80	40	20	10	50
Travel subsidies	50	60	60	90	130	80
School meals and welfare milk	80	20	10	10	-	30
Final income	7,720	9,840	13,690	17,970	28,640	15,570

1 Equivalised disposable income has been used for ranking the households into quintile groups.
2 After tax relief at source on mortgage interest and life assurance premiums.
3 Employees' national insurance contributions.
4 Gross council tax, rates and water charges. Rates in Northern Ireland.

Source: Office for National Statistics

From: Social Trends 1996, Table 5.14

9.7 Percentage of income paid in income tax and national insurance contributions[1]: by marital status and level of earnings[2]

United Kingdom   Percentages

	1971-72	1981-82	1991-92	1995-96[3]
Single man				
Half average earnings				
Tax	14.3	17.5	12.8	11.7
NIC	7.7	7.7	6.2	6.9
Average earnings				
Tax	22.2	23.7	18.9	18.3
NIC	5.8	7.7	7.6	8.5
Twice average earnings				
Tax	26.2	27.3	22.0	23.3
NIC	3.3	6.1	6.0	6.6
Married man[4]				
Half average earnings				
Tax	7.5	10.5	6.5	8.4
NIC	7.7	7.7	6.2	6.9
Average earnings				
Tax	18.8	20.2	15.7	16.7
NIC	5.8	7.7	7.6	8.5
Twice average earnings				
Tax	26.8	25.1	20.4	22.5
NIC	3.3	6.1	6.0	6.6

1 Employees' contributions. Assumes contributions at Class 1, contracted in, standard rate.
2 Average earnings for full-time adult male manual employees working a full week on adult rates.
3 1994-95 based projections.
4 Assuming wife not in paid employment.

Source: Inland Revenue

From: Social Trends 1996, Table 5.11

9.8 Real household disposable income per head

United Kingdom

Thousands

1 Current price figures adjusted to real terms using the consumers' expenditure deflator.

Source: Office for National Statistics

From: Social Trends 1996, Chart 5.1

9.9 Household disposable income: by quintile grouping and household type, 1994-95

United Kingdom   Percentages

	Quintile groups of households[1]					All house-holds
	Bottom fifth	Next fifth	Middle fifth	Next fifth	Top fifth	
Retired households[2]	41	45	24	14	10	27
Non-retired households						
1 adult	12	10	11	14	21	14
2 adults	9	11	19	25	36	20
1 adult with children	14	8	4	2	1	6
2 adults with children	18	18	29	27	22	23
3 or more adults[3]	6	8	13	18	10	11
All households	100	100	100	100	100	100

1 Equivalised disposable income has been used for ranking the households into quintile groups.
2 Households where the combined income of retired members amounts to at least half the total gross income of the household.
3 With or without children.

Source: Office for National Statistics

From: Social Trends 1996, Table 5.15

9.10 Percentage of people whose income is below various fractions of average income[1]

United Kingdom

Percentages

1 Before housing costs.
Source: Institute for Fiscal Studies

From: Social Trends 1996, Chart 5.17

ten

Crime & justice

Definitions and sources

Differences in the legal systems and also in the recording and classification of offences in England and Wales, Scotland and Northern Ireland make it impossible to produce aggregate statistics for the United Kingdom as a whole.

In England and Wales, indictable offences include those which must be tried in the Crown Court and those which may be tried at a magistrates' court or in the Crown Court, although most are actually tried at a magistrates' court. Notifiable offences recorded by the police have a slightly wider definition than indictable offences in that, for example, they also include all criminal damage however small. Standard list offences include all indictable offences plus some summary offences but exclude most summary motoring offences and other less serious summary offences such as drunkenness.

For other sources see: *Guide to Official Statistics, 1996 edition* (520 pages approximately, fully indexed) HMSO.

10.1 Notifiable offences recorded by the police

England and Wales Thousands

	Violence against the person	Sexual offences	Burglary	Robbery	Theft and handling stolen goods	Fraud and forgery	Criminal damage	Other	Total
1990	184.7	29.0	1 006.8	36.2	2 374.4	147.9	733.4	31.1	4 543.6
1991	190.3	29.4	1 219.5	45.3	2 761.1	174.7	821.1	34.6	5 276.2
1992	201.8	29.5	1 355.3	52.9	2 851.6	168.6	892.6	39.4	5 591.7
1993	205.1	31.3	1369.6	57.8	2 751.9	162.8	906.7	41.0	5 526.3
1994	219.2	31.9	1257.9	59.8	2 557.8	145.7	928.6	48.6	5 249.5
1995	217.5	30.4	1 244.2	68.4	2 459.6	134.3	917.0	52.2	5 123.6
1992 Q1	45.5	7.2	347.5	12.0	704.6	42.4	223.8	9.9	1 392.9
Q2	53.4	7.4	313.9	12.4	716.5	42.9	220.5	9.7	1 376.7
Q3	53.1	7.8	316.4	13.6	707.5	42.7	212.1	10.3	1 363.4
Q4	49.8	7.1	377.5	14.8	723.1	40.7	136.3	9.6	1 458.8
1993 Q1	47.2	6.7	380.7	14.2	708.9	42.0	239.6	9.0	1 448.3
Q2	53.2	7.9	336.5	13.7	714.2	41.9	229.2	9.8	1 406.4
Q3	54.1	8.8	315.6	15.2	687.8	41.9	214.9	11.1	1 349.4
Q4	50.6	7.8	336.8	14.7	641.0	37.0	223.1	11.1	1 322.1
1994 Q1	51.4	7.8	341.5	14.7	651.3	37.8	244.5	11.0	1 360.0
Q2	58.2	8.5	310.6	14.4	652.7	38.0	238.8	12.1	1 333.2
Q3	57.5	8.0	281.5	15.3	625.2	35.2	210.0	13.1	1 245.9
Q4	52.1	7.6	324.3	15.4	628.5	34.8	235.3	12.3	1 310.4
1995 Q1	45.3	7.1	322.7	15.1	595.5	32.9	225.6	11.9	1 256.2
Q2	53.2	7.2	303.9	16.7	618.7	33.9	237.3	12.8	1 283.7
Q3	59.6	8.4	291.1	18.3	615.1	33.2	218.5	14.2	1 258.3
Q4	59.4	7.7	326.4	18.3	630.3	34.3	235.6	13.4	1 325.4

Source: Home Office

From: Monthly Digest of Statistics, May 1996, Table 5.1

10.2 Notifiable offences recorded by the police: by type of offence, 1981 and 1994

Thousands

	England & Wales		Scotland		Northern Ireland	
	1981	1994	1981	1994	1981	1994[1]
Theft and handling stolen goods,	1,603	2,561	201	235	25	33
of which: theft of vehicles	333	534	33	42	5	9
theft from vehicles	380	844	..	80	7	7
Burglary	718	1,261	96	88	20	17
Fraud and forgery	107	146	21	24	3	5
Violence against the person	100	220	8	14	3	5
Criminal damage[2]	387	930	62	89	5	3
Robbery	20	60	4	5	3	2
Sexual offences,	19	32	2	4	-	1
of which: rape	1	5	-	1	-	-
Drug trafficking	..	18	2	6	-	-
Other notifiable offences[3]	9	25	12	62	3	2
All notifiable offences	2,964	5,258	408	527	62	68

1 No longer includes assault on police and communicating false information regarding a bomb hoax. These offences have been removed from the categories 'Violence against the person' and 'Other notifiable offences'.
2 In Northern Ireland excludes criminal damage valued at £200 or less.
3 In Northern Ireland includes 'possession of controlled drugs' and 'offences against the state'.

Source: Home Office; The Scottish Office Home Department; Royal Ulster Constabulary

From: Social Trends 1996, Table 9.3

10.3 Offenders found guilty of, or cautioned for, indictable offences[1]: by gender, age and type of offence, 1994

England & Wales

Percentages

	Males					Females				
	10-13	14-17	18-20	21 and over	All aged 10 and over	10-13	14-17	18-20	21 and over	All aged 10 and over
Theft and handling stolen goods	60	47	36	37	40	85	72	62	61	66
Other indictable offences	2	6	15	21	16	1	4	14	18	12
Drug offences	1	10	22	16	15	1	4	11	9	7
Violence against the person	10	13	10	13	12	8	14	9	9	10
Burglary	18	17	13	8	11	3	3	2	1	2
Criminal damage	6	4	3	3	3	1	2	1	1	1
Sexual offences	1	1	1	2	2	0	0	0	0	0
Robbery	2	2	1	1	1	1	1	0	0	-
All indictable offences (=100%)(thousands)	22.8	80.6	75.3	248.1	426.8	9.4	23.0	12.3	51.0	95.7

Source: Home Office

From: Social Trends 1996, Table 9.6

10.4 Victims of crime[1]: by ethnic group, 1993

England & Wales   Percentages

	White	Afro-Caribbean	Asian	All ethnic groups
Household offences				
Home vandalism	4.3	3.9	4.8	4.3
Burglary	6.3	12.9	8.0	6.5
Vehicle crime (owners)				
Vandalism	8.1	12.1	9.8	8.2
All thefts	19.6	25.7	23.0	19.7
Other	10.2	9.5	8.9	10.1
All household offences	32.6	36.2	34.3	32.6
Personal offences				
Assaults	3.8	6.6	3.1	3.8
Threats	3.5	4.0	3.2	3.4
Robbery/theft from person	1.7	2.7	3.4	1.8
Other personal theft	3.7	5.2	3.2	3.7
All personal offences[2]	8.5	13.2	9.3	8.6

1 Percentage in each ethnic group who had been a victim once or more.
2 Excludes sexual offences.

Source: British Crime Survey, Home Office

From: Social Trends 1996, Table 9.10

10.5 Clear-up rates for notifiable offences[1]: by type of offence, 1981 and 1994

Percentages

	England & Wales		Scotland		Northern Ireland	
	1981	1994	1981	1994	1981	1994[1]
Sexual offences,	73	76	65	80	71	89
of which: rape	68	74	74	79	45	69
Drug trafficking[2]	..	102	99	100	100	87
Violence against the person	75	77	83	77	47	67
Fraud and forgery	70	52	78	79	66	65
Theft and handling stolen goods,	38	24	28	26	27	31
of which: theft of vehicles	28	19	26	24	14	19
theft from vehicles	23	13	..	14	12	8
Criminal damage[3]	27	17	22	20	17	36
Burglary	30	21	20	17	22	20
Robbery	25	22	26	29	15	20
Other notifiable offences[4]	91	94	90	98	33	88
All notifiable offences	38	26	31	37	27	36

1 No longer includes assault on police and communicating false information regarding a bomb hoax. These offences have been removed from the categories 'Violence against the person' and 'Other notifiable offences'.
2 In England and Wales offences cleared up in 1994 may have been initially recorded in an earlier year.
3 In Northern Ireland excludes criminal damage valued at £200 or less.
4 In Northern Ireland includes 'possession of controlled drugs' and 'offences against the state'.

Source: Home Office; The Scottish Office Home Department; Royal Ulster Constabulary

From: Social Trends 1996, Table 9.17

10.6 Offenders sentenced for indictable offences[1]: by type of offence and type of sentence[2], 1994

England, Wales & Northern Ireland
Percentages

| | Discharge | Fine | Community sentence | Fully suspended sentence | Immediate custody | | | All sentenced (=100%) |
					Under 5 years	5 years and over	Other	(thousands)
Theft and handling stolen goods	26	32	29	1	11	-	1	124.5
Violence against the person	22	17	32	2	20	2	5	39.1
Burglary	11	8	45	1	34	-	1	38.9
Motoring	15	53	14	1	12	-	5	38.9
Drug offences	16	52	16	1	12	2	-	28.3
Fraud and forgery	22	25	34	2	14	-	2	19.0
Criminal damage	29	19	32	2	10	1	8	11.1
Robbery	4	1	24	1	49	16	5	5.1
Sexual offences	10	13	27	3	33	11	3	4.6
Other	7	65	15	1	12	-	1	12.3
All indictable offences	20	31	28	1	16	1	2	321.8

Source: Home Office; Northern Ireland Office

From: Social Trends 1996, Table 9.14

10.7 People commencing criminal supervision orders[1]

England & Wales
Thousands

	1981	1986	1991	1993	1994
Community service	28	35	42	48	50
Probation	36	40	45	43	49
Combination	.	.	.	9	12
Under the Children and Young Persons Act 1969	12	6	2	2	2
Other	7	7	8	5	5
All persons commencing supervision orders[2]	79	83	91	100	111

1 Supervised by the probation service.
2 Individual figures do not sum to the total because each person may have more than one type of order.
Source: Home Office

From: Social Trends 1996, Table 9.23

10.8 Prison population[1] and accommodation[2]

Great Britain
Thousands

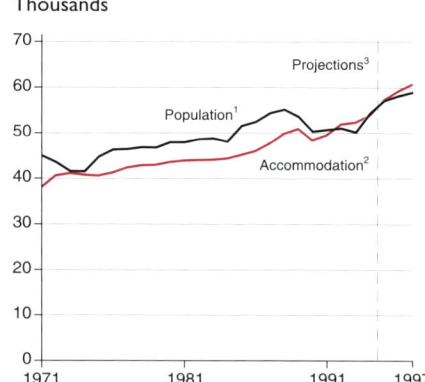

1 Includes those held in police cells in England and Wales from 1980.
2 Certified Normal Accommodation in England and Wales from 1993 excludes accommodation which is not yet operational.
3 At Spring 1995.
Source: Home Office; The Scottish Office Home Department

From: Social Trends 1996, Table 9.19

10.9 Receptions under sentence[1] into prison service establishments

England & Wales

Thousands

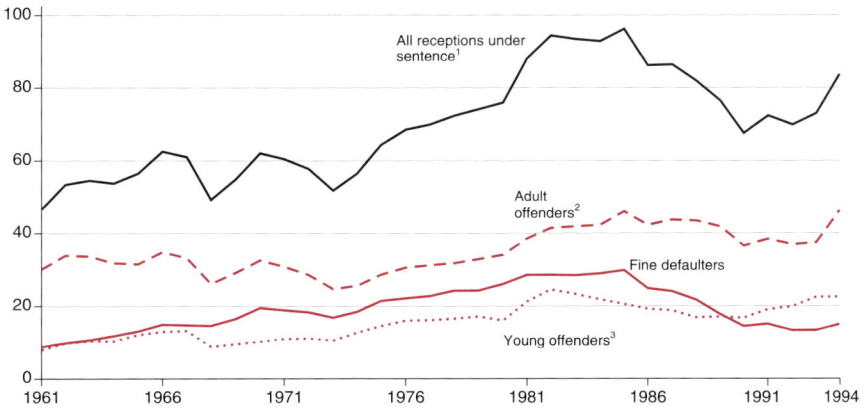

1 Excludes non-criminal prisoners.
2 Includes approved places; excludes fine defaulters.
3 Excludes fine defaulters.

Source: Home Office

From: Social Trends 1996, Chart 9.18

10.10 Average sentence length for adults[1] sentenced at the Crown Court: by gender and type of offence

England & Wales   Months

	Males			Females		
	1981	1991	1994	1981	1991	1994
Drug offences	26	33	30	19	37	35
Sexual offences	28	38	39	20	29	33
Robbery	39	48	50	21	34	31
Criminal damage	19	22	28	14	24	30
Violence against the person	17	20	23	13	20	21
Burglary	17	16	17	11	13	15
Fraud and forgery	16	16	15	10	12	11
Theft and handling stolen goods	11	10	11	7	8	9
Motoring offences	6	8	9	4	9	7
Other	11	12	12	11	14	10
All offences	17	21	22	11	18	18

1 Defendants aged 21 and over sentenced to immediate custody; excludes life sentences.
Source: Home Office

From: Social Trends 1996, Table 9.16

10.11 Complaints against the police

England, Wales & Northern Ireland   Percentages

	1986	1991	1993	1994
Withdrawn/not proceeded with	39	42	41	41
Informally resolved[1]	12	23	27	31
Investigated				
Unsubstantiated	45	33	30	26
Substantiated	4	2	2	2
All complaints (=100%) (thousands)	32.6	39.7	39.3	41.2

1 Not applicable to Northern Ireland in 1986.

Source: Home Office; Royal Ulster Constabulary

From: Social Trends 1996, Table 9.26

10.12 Employment in the criminal justice system[1]

Great Britain

	Thousands				Rates per 10,000 population	
	1971	1981	1991	1994	1971	1994
Police service						
Police	108	133	141	141	19.9	22.8
Civilian staff[2]	36	45	55	60	6.7	9.7
All police service	144	178	196	201	26.6	32.5
Prison service[3]	17	24	33	38	3.5	7.4
Probation service[4]	..	12	18	17	..	3.2

1 At December each year.
2 Includes traffic wardens, clerical and technical staff.
3 England and Wales only. Prior to 1993 excludes headquarters staff and prison officer class trainees.
4 England and Wales only. Full-time plus part-time workers and includes some temporary officers and also some trainees from 1981 onwards. Excludes non-probation officer grade hostel staff.

Source: Home Office; The Scottish Office Home Department

From: Social Trends 1996, Table 9.28

eleven

Environment

Definitions and sources

The main source of national trend data on the state of the environment in the UK is the annual *Digest of Environmental Protection and Water Statistics*. Definitional notes and guidance on further sources are given as footnotes to the tables.

For other sources see: *Guide to Official Statistics, 1996 edition* (520 pages approximately, fully indexed) HMSO.

Digest of Environmental Protection and Water Statistics, HMSO.

11.1 Recycling levels: by material

United Kingdom					Percentages
	1991	1992	1993	1994	2000 (target)
Paper and board	34	34	32	33	..
Waste paper used in newsprint	26	31	31	33	40
Glass	21	26	29	28	50
Aluminium cans	11	16	21	24	50
Steel cans	10	12	13	14	37
Plastics	..	5	..	..	..

Source: ACRA; BGMC; BP&BIF; BS; SCRIB; PFGB; PPIC

From: Social Trends 1996, Table 11.3

11.2 Air pollutants: emissions of selected gases

United Kingdom

Million tonnes

Carbon monoxide
Sulphur dioxide
Nitrogen oxides
Black smoke

Source: National Environmental Technology Centre

From: Social Trends 1996, Chart 11.1

11.3 Air pollutants: by source, 1994

United Kingdom — Percentages

	Carbon dioxide	Carbon monoxide	Sulphur dioxide	Nitrogen oxides	Volatile organic compounds	Black smoke
Road transport	20	88	2	49	29	58
Electricity supply	30	-	65	24	-	4
Domestic	15	7	3	3	2	22
Other	35	5	30	24	69	15
All air pollutants (=100%)						
(million tonnes)	149.0	4.8	2.7	2.2	2.1	0.4

Source: National Environmental Technology Centre

From: Social Trends 1996, Table 11.9

11.4 Biological and chemical water quality of rivers and canals

Percentages and kilometres

	1990 Biological quality[1] (percentages)				Total surveyed length (=100%) (kms)	1992-1994[2] Chemical quality[3] (percentages)				Total surveyed length (=100%) (kms)
	Good	Moderate	Poor	Very poor		Good	Fair	Poor	Bad	
United Kingdom	64	21	9	6	48,680	..	..	..	..	..
North West	46	15	13	26	4,170	53	31	13	3	5,740
Northumbria & Yorkshire[4]	65	15	11	9	6,100	63	22	14	1	5,320
Severn Trent	37	30	22	10	5,320	43	45	10	1	6,370
Anglian	52	33	11	3	5,990	35	52	12	1	4,650
Thames	68	16	11	6	3,430	54	42	4	-	3,780
Southern	72	17	8	3	1,920	55	38	6	-	2,210
South Western[4]	79	15	5	1	4,770	74	23	3	-	6,040
England	58	21	12	9	31,700	54	35	9	1	34,110
Wales[5]	77	17	5	1	3,850	89	9	2	-	5,040
Scotland	78	18	2	1	10,870	..	..	..	..	..
Northern Ireland[6]	54	34	10	2	2,250	..	..	..	..	..

1 Classification based on the River Invertebrate Prediction and Classification System (RIVPACS).
2 Average of three years' data combined.
3 Based on the chemical quality grade of the General Quality Assessment (GQA) scheme.
4 In 1993, the Northumbria and Yorkshire regions amalgamated, as did the Wessex and South West regions.
5 NRA Welsh Region, the boundary of which does not coincide with the boundary of Wales.
6 Figures from the 1991 Biological Survey.

Source: Department of the Environment; National Rivers Authority; The Scottish Office Development Department; Department of the Environment, Northern Ireland

From: Regional Trends 1996, Table 11.2

11.5   Fish stocks[1]: by sea area and selected species

United Kingdom					Thousand tonnes
	1990	1991	1992	1993	1994
North Sea					
Cod	63	62	60	57	59
Haddock	69	62	103	133	158
Sole	93	81	82	58	82
Herring[2]	1,154	998	775	492	792
Whiting	303	259	256	249	256
Plaice	398	340	325	284	252
West of Scotland					
Cod	18	16	13	15	15
Haddock	25	23	31	50	49
Western English Channel					
Sole	3	3	3	3	3
Mackerel[3]	2,684	3,028	2,937	2,474	2,035

1 Spawning stock biomass.
2 Includes Eastern English Channel.
3 Western stock.

Source: International Council for the Exploration of the Sea

From: Social Trends 1996, Table 11.21

11.6   Actual abstractions from all surface and groundwater sources: by purpose

England & Wales				Ml/day
	1991	1992	1993	1994
Public water supply[1]	17,563	17,957	16,651	16,735
Spray irrigation	365	284	163	285
Agriculture[2]	134	127	140	119
Electricity supply industry	30,361	38,304	26,579	27,732
Other industry	5,472	4,716	3,895	4,292
Mineral washing	172	212	198	223
Fish farming	3,883	4,475	3,817	3,983
Private water supply	..	51	82	85
Other	1,254	1,795	93	196
All abstractions	59,203	67,921	51,618	53,650

1 Includes some private water supply for 1991.
2 Excludes spray irrigation.

Source: National Rivers Authority; Department of the Environment

From: Social Trends 1996, Table 11.20

11.7 Production of primary fuels

United Kingdom

Million tonnes of oil equivalent

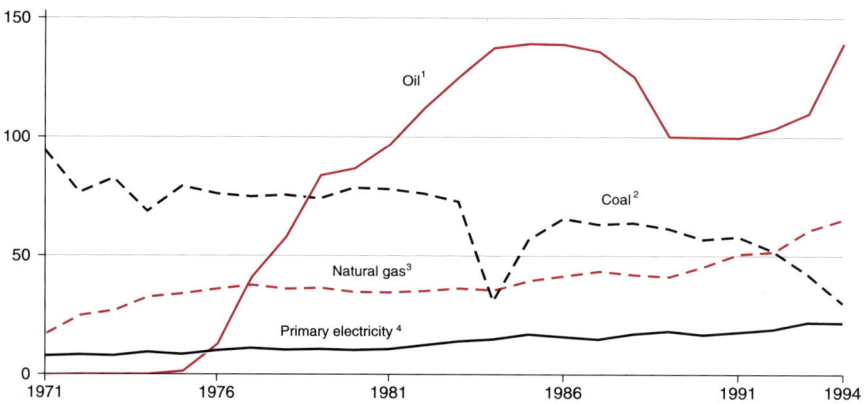

1 Includes crude oil, natural gas liquids and feedstocks.
2 From 1988 includes solid renewables (wood, straw, waste, etc).
3 Includes colliery methane and, from 1988, landfill gas and sewage gas.
4 Nuclear, natural flow hydro-electricity and, from 1988, generation at wind stations.

Source: Department of Trade and Industry

From: Social Trends 1996, Chart 11.23

twelve

Transport

Definitions and sources

The traffic figures for Great Britain were revised in 1989 (see *Road Traffic in Great Britain: Review of Estimates, Transport Statistics Report,* HMSO 1989). The figures are compiled using roadside traffic counts from which estimates of average daily flow are made. These are combined with information on road lengths to provide estimates of traffic volume in terms of vehicle kilometres.

For other sources see: *Guide to Official Statistics, 1996 edition* (520 pages approximately, fully indexed) HMSO.
Transport Statistics, Great Britain, HMSO.

12.1 Mode of transport[1]: by purpose, 1992-1994

Great Britain   Percentages

	Car/van	Rail[2]	Local bus	Walk	Motor-cycle	Bicycle	Other	All modes
Commuting	18	49	20	9	48	38	11	19
Business	6	7	1	1	4	3	4	5
Education	2	7	14	10	1	10	19	5
Shopping	19	9	33	23	12	11	10	20
Other personal business	24	7	12	14	8	9	14	21
Leisure	31	21	20	44	27	29	41	31
All purposes	100	100	100	100	100	100	100	100

1 Percentage of journey stages. Excludes journeys under one mile.
2 Includes London Underground.

Source: National Travel Survey, Department of Transport

From: Social Trends 1996, Table 12.5

12.2 Passenger transport in Great Britain: estimated passenger kilometres

Thousand million passenger kilometres

	1984	1985	1986	1987	1988	1989	1990	1991	1992	1993	1994[5]
Air[1]	3	4	4	4	5	5	5	5	5	5	5
Rail[2]	35	37	37	40	41	40	40	38	38	37	35
Road:											
Public service vehicles[3]	48	49	47	47	46	47	46	44	43	43	43
Cars and vans[4,6,7]	432	441	465	500	536	581	588	584	587	585	596
Motor cycles[4,6]	9	8	8	7	6	6	6	6	5	4	4
Pedal cycles	6	6	5	6	5	5	5	5	5	5	5
Total	534	544	566	604	639	684	690	682	682	679	689

1 Domestic scheduled and non-scheduled services, including Northern Ireland, Isle of Man and Channel Islands.
2 British Rail, London Regional Transport and Passenger Transport Executive railway systems. The basis of calculating London Regional Transport railways' passenger kilometres has been revised from passenger kilometres paid for to passenger kilometres travelled.
3 Calculated from operators' returns of numbers of passengers carried, using estimates for average length of journey.
4 Based on statistics of vehicle mileage derived from the traffic counts and estimates of average numbers of persons per vehicle, derived from the National Travel surveys.
5 Provisional figures.
6 In 1993 the occupancy rates, estimated from the National Travel Survey, were 1.66 for cars and taxis and 1.075 for motor cycles.
7 Includes taxis.

Source: Department of Transport

From: Annual Abstract of Statistics 1996, Table 10.2.

12.3 Motor vehicles currently licensed as at 31 December 1985 - 1995[1]

Thousands

	Private and light goods		Motorcycles, scooters and mopeds	Public transport vehicles[3]	Goods vehicles[2,4]	Agricultural tractors[5]	Other vehicles[6]	Crown and exempt vehicles	All vehicles
	Private cars[2]	Other vehicles[2]							
1985	16 453	1 804	1 148	120	486	374	77	695	21 157
1986	16 981	1 879	1 065	125	484	371	72	720	21 699
1987	17 421	1 952	978	129	484	374	68	744	22 152
1988	18 432	2 095	912	132	503	383	83	761	23 302
1989	19 248	2 199	875	122	505	384	77	785	24 196
1990	19 742	2 247	833	115	482	376	71	807	24 673
1991	19 737	2 215	750	109	449	346	65	840	24 511
1992	19 870	2 198	684	107	432	324	59	903	24 577
1993	20 102	2 187	650	107	428	318	55	979	24 826
1994	20 479	2 192	630	107	434	309	50	1 030	25 231
1995	20 505	2 217	594	74[7]	421	274[8]	114	1 170	25 369

1 For the years up to 1992, estimates are taken from the annual vehicle census analyses based on the Driver and Vehicle Licensing Agency main vehicle file. From 1992, estimates of licensed stock are taken from the Department of Transport's Statistics Directorate Vehicle Information Database.
2 For years up to 1990 retrospective counts within these new taxation classes have been estimated.
3 Includes taxis.
4 Includes agricultural vans and lorries and showmen's goods vehicles licensed to draw trailers.
5 Includes combine hearvesters, mowing machines, digging machines, mobile cranes and works trucks.
6 Incudes three-wheelers, pedestrian controlled vehicles and showmen's haulage.
7 Taxation group now restricted to only vehicles with 9 or more seats.
8 Taxation group subject to revision from 1 July 1995, now termed "special concessions group".

Source: Department of Transport

From: Monthly Digest of Statistics, May 1996, Table 13.2.

12.4 Index numbers of road traffic and goods transport by road

Average 1977 = 100

		Index of vehicle kilometres travelled on road in Great Britain								Index of tonne-kilo-metres of road goods transport[3,4,5]
		Motor traffic								
		All motor traffic	Motor cycles etc	Cars and taxis	Buses and coaches	Light vans[1]	Other goods vehicles Total	Articulated[2]	Pedal cycles	
1988		152	97	157	134	145	129	158	86	131
1989		165	96	171	140	160	137	174	86	139
1990		166	90	173	142	161	134	171	87	137
1991		166	87	173	149	168	134	171	86	131
1992		167	73	174	144	166	133	163	78	128
1993		167	67	174	144	165	134	164	74	135
1994		171	67	178	147	173	140	177	72	145
1995		174	..	181	..	177	142	176	..	151
1993	Q1	152	49	160	135	145	125	143	62	138
	Q2	170	69	179	154	168	131	156	82	133
	Q3	179	87	186	150	180	144	181	94	135
	Q4	166	61	173	137	168	136	175	56	135
1994	Q1	158	60	165	143	161	131	167	45	145
	Q2	174	74	181	155	176	141	175	83	145
	Q3	181	74	189	152	185	147	185	101	145
	Q4	169	60	177	139	172	140	182	59	144
1995	Q1	163	..	170	..	167	134	172	..	149
	Q2	175	..	182	..	179	142	175	..	149
	Q3	184	..	192	..	186	147	180	..	157
	Q4	172	..	180	..	176	144	181	..	150

1 Not exceeding 3,500 kgs gross vehicle weight.
2 Includes vehicles with drawbar trailers.
3 The figures for road goods transport are estimated from a continuing sample enquiry.
4 The quarterly figures relate to 13-week periods and not three calendar months.
5 Revised to exclude estimates of work done by vehicles under 3.5 tonnes gross vehicle weight.

Source: Department of Transport

From: Monthly Digest of Statistics, May 1996, Table 13.3.

12.5 Households with regular use of a car[1]: by socio-economic group[2], 1994-95

Great Britain   Percentages

	None	One car only	Two or more cars
Professional	5	40	55
Employers and managers	4	40	55
Intermediate non-manual	15	56	29
Junior non-manual	28	54	18
Skilled manual and own account non-professional	14	54	32
Semi-skilled manual and personal service	33	53	14
Unskilled manual	45	47	8
Economically inactive	55	38	7
All groups	31	45	24

1 Or van.
2 Of head of household. Excludes members of the Armed Forces, economically active full-time students and those who were unemployed and had never worked.

Source: General Household Survey, Office for National Statistics

From: Social Trends 1996, Table 12.7

12.6 Local (stage) bus services: vehicle kilometres and passenger journeys

Great Britain

Millions

	London[1]	English metropolitan areas	English shire counties	England	Scotland	Wales	All Great Britain	All outside London	All outside London and English metropolitan areas
Vehicle kilometres									
1988/89	285	634	1 027	1 946	325	118	2 390	2 104	1 470
1989/90	292	654	1 041	1 987	336	119	2 442	2 150	1 496
1990/91	304	650	1 035	1 989	336	123	2 448	2 144	1 494
1991/92	316	662	1 035	2 013	355	120	2 488	2 172	1 510
1992/93	330	679	1 040	2 049	347	119	2 515	2 185	1 506
1993/94	343	693	1 058	2 095	361	130	2 585	2 242	1 549
1994/95	356	739	1 086	2 181	369	125	2 676	2 320	1 581
Passenger journeys									
1988/89	1 211	1 695	1 501	4 407	647	161	5 215	4 004	2 309
1989/90	1 188	1 648	1 474	4 310	613	151	5 074	3 886	2 238
1990/91	1 178	1 547	1 396	4 120	585	145	4 850	3 672	2 126
1991/92	1 149	1 478	1 333	3 961	571	133	4 665	3 516	2 038
1992/93	1 129	1 383	1 307	3 819	532	129	4 480	3 351	1 968
1993/94	1 117	1 337	1 274	3 727	525	133	4 386	3 268	1 931
1994/95	1 167	1 331	1 277	3 775	513	132	4 420	3 253	1 922

1 Passenger journey statistics for London may not be consistent with those published by London Regional Transport.

Source: Department of Transport

From: Monthly Digest of Statistics, May 1996, Table 13.5.

12.7 British Rail and London Underground

Millions

		British Rail: passenger kilometres			London Underground: passenger journeys		
		Ordinary fares	Season tickets	Total	Full and reduced fares	Season tickets	Total
1989/90		22 750	10 898	33 647	380	385	765
1990/91		22 803	10 389	33 191	398	377	775
1991/92		22 435	10 032	32 466	368	383	751
1992/93		22 281	9 438	31 718	366	365	729
1993/94		21 331	9 024	30 357	376	360	735
1994/95		20 658	7 996	28 655	398	365	764
1992	Q1	5 033	2 614	7 646	86	97	183
	Q2	5 646	2 295	7 941	90	90	179
	Q3	6 034	2 172	8 206	96	89	184
	Q4	5 442	2 497	7 938	93	92	185
1993	Q1	5 159	2 474	7 633	87	94	181
	Q2	5 169	2 111	7 280	91	87	177
	Q3	5 841	2 071	7 913	97	88	185
	Q4	5 326	2 417	7 744	94	91	185
1994	Q1	4 995	2 425	7 420	94	94	188
	Q2[1]	5 289	2 034	7 323	95	89	184
	Q3[1]	4 874	1 677	6 552	101	88	189
	Q4	5 443	2 114	7 557	105	94	199
1995	Q1	5 052	2 171	7 223	97	94	192
	Q2[2]	5 527	1 907	7 434	101	89	190
	Q3[1,2]	5 797	1 676	7 473	106	91	197
	Q4[2]	5 634	2 030	7 665	109	93	202

1 British Rail figures affected by industrial action.
2 Provisional.

Source: Department of Transport

From: Monthly Digest of Statistics, May 1996, Table 13.7

12.8 Passenger car arrivals at, and departures from, UK ports: by overseas country

Thousands

	1981	1986	1991	1993	1994
By ship					
France	1,402	1,944	3,329	4,058	4,575
Irish Republic	378	345	611	621	634
Belgium	591	478	514	413	404
Netherlands	259	325	399	410	328
Spain and Portugal	20	27	47	70	79
Germany	22	21	34	44	48
Scandinavia and Baltic	62	67	56	53	42
Denmark	50	45	44	32	39
All overseas routes	2,784	3,252	5,034	5,701	6,148
By hovercraft					
France	287	218	189	158	181
All overseas routes	3,071	3,470	5,223	5,859	6,330

Source: Department of Transport

From: Social Trends 1996, Table 12.12

12.9 Domestic[1] and international air passengers: by selected airport

United Kingdom Thousands

	Domestic				International			
	1972	1981	1991	1994	1971	1981	1991	1994
Heathrow	2,947	3,867	6,714	7,106	13,437	22,543	33,531	44,261
Gatwick	588	1,011	1,012	1,628	4,143	9,714	17,679	19,417
Manchester	707	983	1,906	2,269	1,419	3,729	8,196	12,064
Birmingham	303	378	720	838	553	1,091	2,526	3,946
Glasgow	1,411	1,426	2,289	2,586	415	839	1,865	2,870
Stansted	3	11	253	475	475	253	1,432	2,782
Luton	49	33	210	111	2,668	1,938	1,748	1,692
Newcastle	320	378	544	699	155	564	983	1,718
East Midlands	190	221	342	280	172	518	802	1,335
Bristol	58	44	141	223	150	202	641	1,053
Aberdeen	188	1,037	1,317	1,461	-	515	703	701
Cardiff	..	62	56	74	141	232	457	923
Belfast	1,115	1,220	1,785	1,407	68	170	384	632
Other	2,930	3,368	5,701	6,847	1,332	1,423	1,839	2,966
All airports	10,809	14,039	22,990	26,005	25,128	43,731	72,786	96,359

1 Passengers are recorded at both airport of departure and arrival. Includes British Government/armed forces on official business and travel to/from oil rigs.

Source: Civil Aviation Authority

From: Social Trends 1996, Table 12.14

12.10 International passenger movements: by mode

United Kingdom

Millions

1 Arrivals plus departures.

Source: Department of Transport

From: Social Trends 1996, Chart 12.13

12.11 Car driver casualties: by gender and age

United Kingdom — Percentages

	1986	1991	1994
Males			
17-21	*23*	*22*	*18*
22-39	*45*	*46*	*47*
40-59	*22*	*22*	*23*
60 and over	*11*	*11*	*11*
All males[1] (=100%)			
(thousands)	*61.1*	*66.4*	*70.1*
Females			
17-21	*20*	*20*	*16*
22-39	*49*	*50*	*53*
40-59	*24*	*24*	*25*
60 and over	*7*	*6*	*7*
All females[1] (=100%)			
(thousands)	*32.5*	*45.5*	*54.7*

1 Excludes cases where age of casualty was unknown.

Source: Department of Transport; Royal Ulster Constabulary

From: Social Trends 1996, Table 12.17

12.12 Passenger death rates: by mode of transport

Great Britain — Rates per billion passenger kilometres

	1981	1986	1991	1992	1993	Average 1983-1993
Motorcycle	115.8	100.3	94.4	97.0	94.6	104.0
Foot	76.9	75.3	62.5	58.5	56.2	70.5
Pedal cycle	56.9	49.6	46.8	43.4	41.3	48.8
Water [1]	0.4	0.5	0.0	0.5	0.0	9.2
Car	6.1	5.1	3.7	3.5	3.0	4.6
Van	3.8	3.8	2.2	2.2	1.7	2.7
Rail	1.0	0.9	0.8	0.4	0.4	0.9
Bus or coach	0.3	0.5	0.6	0.4	0.8	0.5
Air [1]	0.2	0.5	0.0	0.1	0.0	0.2

1 Data are for United Kingdom.

Source: Department of Transport

From: Social Trends 1996, Table 12.15

thirteen

Lifestyles & tourism

Definitions and sources

Most of the tables and charts in this section are taken from *Social Trends* 26 which uses data from both government and non-government sources.

For other sources see: *Guide to Official Statistics, 1996 edition* (520 pages approximately, fully indexed) HMSO.

13.1 Time use: by employment status and gender, May 1995

Great Britain — Hours

	In full-time employment		In part-time employment		Retired		All adults
	Males	Females	Males	Females	Males	Females	
Weekly hours spent on							
Sleep	57	58	62	60	67	66	61
Free time	34	31	48	32	59	52	40
Work, study and travel	53	48	28	26	3	4	32
Housework, cooking and shopping	7	15	12	26	15	26	16
Eating, personal hygiene and caring	13	13	13	21	15	17	15
Household maintenance and pet care	4	2	6	3	9	3	4
Free time per weekday	4	4	6	4	8	7	5
Free time per weekend day	8	6	8	6	10	8	8

Source: ESRC Research Centre on Micro-social Change, from Omnibus Survey

From: Social Trends 1996, Table 13.2

13.2 Division of household tasks[1], 1994

Great Britain   Percentages

	Always the woman	Usually the woman	About equal or both together	Usually the man	Always the man	All couples[2]
Washing and ironing	47	32	18	1	1	100
Deciding what to have for dinner	27	32	35	3	1	100
Looking after sick family members	22	26	45	..	..	100
Shopping for groceries	20	21	52	4	1	100
Small repairs around the house	2	3	18	49	25	100

1 By married couples or couples living as married.
2 Includes those who did not answer and where the task was done by a third person.
Source: British Social Attitudes Survey, Social & Community Planning Research

From: Social Trends 1996, Table 13.3

13.3 Participation[1] in home-based leisure activities: by gender and age, 1993-94

Great Britain   Percentages

	16-19	20-24	25-29	30-44	45-59	60-69	70 and over	All aged 16 and over
Males								
Watching TV	99	100	99	99	99	99	97	99
Visiting/entertaining								
friends or relations	96	97	97	97	94	94	91	95
Listening to radio	93	95	95	94	91	86	83	91
Listening to records/tapes	96	96	93	86	76	66	50	79
Reading books	55	58	56	60	61	59	58	59
Gardening	24	22	37	52	62	65	55	51
DIY	34	44	61	68	65	58	35	57
Dressmaking/needlework/								
knitting	2	3	3	3	3	3	4	3
Females								
Watching TV	99	99	99	99	99	99	98	99
Visiting/entertaining								
friends or relations	98	98	99	98	96	95	94	96
Listening to radio	97	95	92	91	88	84	77	88
Listening to records/tapes	97	96	92	88	75	62	42	75
Reading books	75	70	70	71	71	74	67	71
Gardening	11	23	34	51	57	54	39	45
DIY	16	35	39	40	34	23	10	30
Dressmaking/needlework/								
knitting	19	30	30	37	44	48	38	38

1 Percentage in each age group participating in each activity in the four weeks before interview.
Source: General Household Survey, Office for National Statistics

From: Social Trends 1996, Table 13.7

13.4 Radio listening: by age, 1994

United Kingdom	Hours and minutes per week
	1994
4-15	5:54
16-34	17:19
35-64	18:17
65 and over	18:07
All aged 4 and over	16:07
Reach[1] (percentages)	
Daily	67
Weekly	84

1 Percentage of the population aged 4 and over who listened to the radio for at least half a programme a day.

Source: British Broadcasting Corporation

From: Social Trends 1996, Table 13.6

13.5 Trade deliveries of LPs, cassettes, CDs and singles[1]

United Kingdom

Millions of units

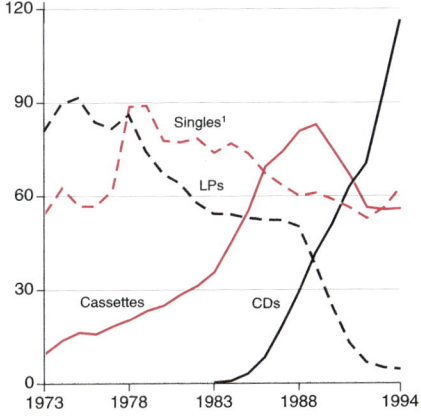

1 All formats combined (7",12", cassette and CD).

Source: British Phonographic Industry

From: Social Trends 1996, Chart 13.8

13.6 Reading of national daily newspapers: by age and gender, January-December 1995

Great Britain   Percentages

	Percentage reading each paper							Readership[1] (millions)	Readers per copy (numbers)
	15-24	25-44	45-64	65 and over	Males	Females	All adults		
The Sun	30	25	19	16	26	19	22	10.2	2.6
Daily Mirror	14	13	14	15	16	13	14	6.5	2.7
Daily Mail	8	8	12	11	10	9	10	4.4	2.5
Daily Express	5	5	8	9	7	7	7	3.1	2.5
The Daily Telegraph	4	5	8	7	7	5	6	2.7	2.7
Daily Star	7	6	4	2	7	3	5	2.1	3.3
The Times	4	4	4	3	4	3	4	1.6	2.7
The Guardian	3	3	4	1	3	2	3	1.3	3.5
The Independent	2	2	2	1	2	2	2	1.0	3.2
Financial Times	1	2	2	1	2	1	2	0.7	4.3
Any national daily newspaper[2]	56	55	61	60	62	54	58	26.6	..

1 Defined as the average issue readership and represents the number of people who claim to have read or looked at one or more copies of a given publication during a period equal to the interval at which the publication appears.
2 Includes the above newspapers plus the Daily Record, Sporting Life and Racing Post.

Source: National Readership Surveys Ltd

From: Social Trends 1996, Table 13.9

13.7 The most popular magazines and newspapers read[1] by children: by age and gender, 1995

United Kingdom   Percentages

Aged 7-10		Aged 11-14	
Males		**Males**	
Beano	28	The Sun	22
Match	25	Match	18
Shoot!	22	Shoot!	18
Sonic the Comic	18	News of the World	17
Dandy	17	Beano	15
Females		**Females**	
Smash Hits	16	Just Seventeen	41
Barbie	13	Sugar	39
Girl talk	13	Big!	34
Beano	12	It's Bliss	34
Live and Kicking	12	Smash Hits	32

1 For 7 to 10 year olds data are the percentage of children who said they read the publication; for 11 to 14 year olds data are the average issue readership.

Source: Youth TGI, BMRB International

From: Social Trends 1996, Table 13.11

13.8 Participation[1] in leisure activities away from home: by gender, 1994-95

Great Britain   Percentages

	Males	Females	All persons
Meal in a restaurant (not fast food)	60	64	62
Drive for pleasure	47	47	47
Meal in a fast food restaurant	45	40	42
Library	36	43	40
Cinema	35	32	34
Short break holiday	32	28	30
Disco or night club	29	22	25
Historic building	27	24	25
Spectator sports event	31	13	22
Theatre	19	22	21

1 Percentage of the population aged 16 and over participating in each activity in the three months prior to interview.

Source: The Henley Centre

From: Social Trends 1996, Table 13.13

13.9 Participation[1] in the most popular sports, games and physical activities: by gender and age, 1993-94

United Kingdom   Percentages

	16-19	20-24	25-29	30-44	45-59	60-69	70 and over	All aged 16 and over
Males								
Walking	45	46	48	48	47	45	33	45
Snooker/pool/billiards	56	47	34	23	14	8	3	21
Swimming	23	19	19	21	12	8	3	15
Cycling	37	19	21	16	11	6	5	14
Soccer	44	27	19	9	2	0	0	9
Golf	15	13	12	11	9	7	3	9
Females								
Walking	40	41	41	41	42	36	20	37
Keep fit/yoga	29	28	26	22	14	8	6	17
Swimming	26	25	22	24	14	8	3	16
Cycling	14	12	8	9	7	4	2	7
Snooker/pool/billiards	26	17	6	4	2	1	0	5
Tenpin bowls/skittles	9	9	5	4	2	1	0	3

1 Percentage in each age group participating in each activity in the four weeks before interview.

Source: General Household Survey, Office for National Statistics; Continuous Household Survey, Department of Finance and Personnel, Northern Ireland

From: Social Trends 1996, Table 13.17

13.10 Holidays[1]: by number taken per year by Great Britain residents

Percentages

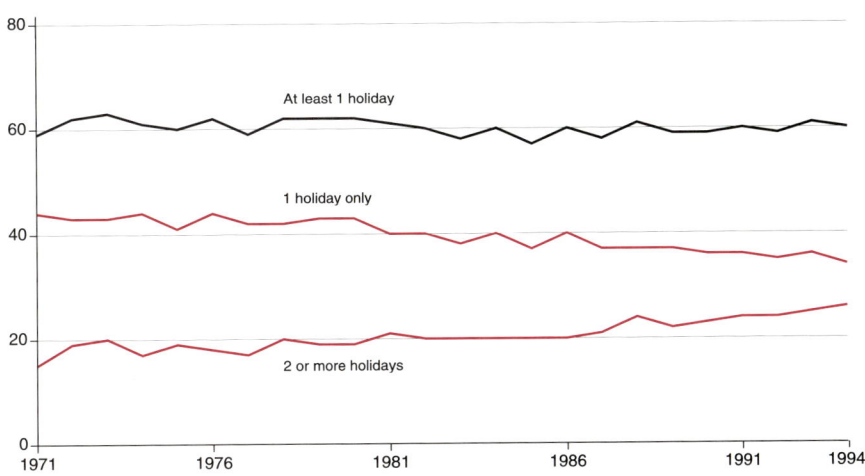

1 Holidays of four nights or more taken by Great Britain residents aged 16 and over. Includes domestic and foreign holidays.

Source: British National Travel Survey, British Tourist Authority

From: Social Trends 1996, Chart 13.1

13.11 Holidays[1] taken at home by Great Britain residents: by destination, 1994

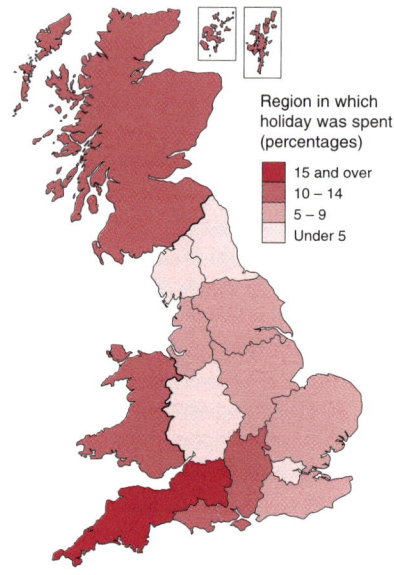

Region in which holiday was spent (percentages)

- 15 and over
- 10 – 14
- 5 – 9
- Under 5

1 Holidays of four nights or more taken by adults aged 16 and over.

Source: British National Travel Survey, British Tourist Authority

From: Social Trends 1996, Chart 13.21

13.12 Destination of holidays[1] abroad

Percentages

	1971	1981	1991	1994
Spain[2]	34.3	21.7	21.3	26.4
France	15.9	27.2	25.8	22.2
Greece	4.5	6.7	7.6	7.6
United States	1.0	5.5	6.8	5.7
Portugal	2.6	2.8	4.8	3.9
Italy	9.2	5.8	3.5	3.9
Cyprus	1.0	0.7	2.4	3.3
Irish Republic	..	3.6	3.0	2.7
Netherlands	3.6	2.4	3.5	2.6
Turkey	..	0.1	0.7	2.4
Germany	3.4	2.6	2.7	2.0
Austria	5.5	2.5	2.4	1.8
Other countries	19.0	18.4	15.6	15.4
All destinations (=100%) (thousands)	4,201	13,131	20,788	27,336

1 A visit made for holiday purposes. Business trips and visits to friends or relatives are excluded.
2 Excludes the Canaries prior to 1981.

Source: International Passenger Survey, Office for National Statistics

From: Social Trends 1996, Table 13.22

13.13 Overseas travel and tourism: earnings and expenditure

£ million, current prices, not seasonally adjusted

	Expenditure by overseas visitors to UK	Expenditure by UK residents abroad	Net earnings in UK		Expenditure by overseas visitors to UK	Expenditure by UK residents abroad	Net earnings in UK
1991	7 386	9 951	-2 565	1995 Jan	718	912	-194
1992	7 891	11 243	-3 352	Feb	532	769	-237
1993	9 487	12 972	-3 485	Mar	793	1 034	-241
1994	9 919	14 500	-4 581	Apr	873	1 110	-237
1995	11 885	15 586	-3 700	May	930	1 264	-334
				Jun	1 003	1 596	-593
1994 Q1	1 711	2 583	-872	Jul	1 418	1 647	-229
Q2	2 377	3 553	-1 175	Aug	1 533	2 042	-509
Q3	3 698	5 389	-1 692	Sep	1 241	1 932	-691
Q4	2 134	2 975	-841	Oct	1 029	1 580	-551
				Nov	844	925	-81
1995 Q1	2 043	2 715	-672	Dec	971	775	196
Q2	2 805	3 970	-1 164				
Q3	4 193	5 621	-1 428	1996 Jan	670	980	-310
Q4	2 844	3 280	-436	Feb	635	940	-305

Source: Office for National Statistics

From: Monthly Digest of Statistics, May 1996, Table 19.2.

fourteen

Education

Definitions and sources

Educational establishments in the United Kingdom may be administered and financed in a number of ways.

Public sector: by local education authorities, which form part of the structure of local government;

Assisted: by governing bodies which have a substantial degree of autonomy from public authorities but which receive grants direct from central government sources;

Grant maintained: since 1988 it has been possible for local education authority maintained schools to apply for Grant maintained status and receive direct grants from the apprropriate education department. The governing body of such a school is responsible for all aspects of school management, including the deployment of funds, employment of staff and provision of most educational support services. In January 1995 there were 415 primary and 632 secondary Grant maintained schools in England and Wales plus 1 grant maintained school in Scotland.

Independent: by the private sector, including individuals, companies, and charitable institutions;

Local Management of Schools (LMS): In recent years under the LMS initiative, all public sector and assisted schools have delegated responsibility for managing their school budgets and staff numbers.

The pupil/teacher ratios used here are the ratios of all pupils to all teachers employed on the day of annual count (part-time teachers are included on a full-time equivalent basis). The count is taken in January (September in Scotland from 1974/75, and October in Northern Ireland from 1992/93).

Ages are measured at 31 August for 1980/81 onwards ie. immediately prior to the school academic year, so yielding complete academic year cohorts and in particular correct post-compulsory school age data.

Further education The term 'further education' may be used in a general sense to cover all non-advanced education after the period of compulsory education. More commonly it excludes those staying on at secondary schools, and those studying higher education at universities and other establishments. From 1993 all colleges in the Further Education Funding Councils (FEFC) Sector and further education courses in other establishments have been funded by an FEFC. On 1 April 1993 sixth form colleges were incorporated into the FEFC and have transferred out of the schools sector.

Higher education The term 'higher education' as used here covers all advanced courses (including teacher training courses) in universities and institutions of higher and further education, that is those leading to qualifications above General Certificate of Education 'A' level, Scottish Certificate of Education 'H' grade, BTEC National Diploma and Ordinary National Diploma; or their equivalents. Since April 1993 publicly funded HE courses in the UK have been funded by the HE funding councils, the FE Funding Councils of England and Wales, the Scottish Office Education and Industry Department and the Department of Education, Northern Ireland.

There are very helpful explanatory notes given in *Social Trends* Appendix Part 3, as well as in the publications of the education departments (summarised in bulletins).

Former UFC university students are counted on 31 December as are teacher training students in Northern Ireland. All other students outside former UFC universities were counted on 1 November in England and Wales, and in October in Scotland and for further education in Northern Ireland. From 1994/95 onwards higher education institution students are counted on 31 December except Scotland which is 31 July (full session count).

Full-time includes sandwich courses; part-time includes evening only courses and open distance learning.

For other sources see: *Guide to Official Statistics, 1996 edition* (520 pages approximately, fully indexed) HMSO.

Education Statistics for the United Kingdom, 1994 edition (92 pages approximately, fully indexed) HMSO.

14.1 Adult literacy and numeracy standards[1]: by age on leaving full-time education, 1994

England & Wales   Percentages

	Low literacy	High literacy	Low numeracy	High numeracy
Age on leaving full-time education				
Under 16	14	9	31	11
16	8	19	16	23
17-18	4	30	8	30
19-20	3	31	7	40
21 and over	-	46	3	54
All adults[1]	8	21	18	25

1 Percentage of adults aged 22 to 74.

Source: Basic Skills Agency

From: Social Trends 1996, Table 3.2

14.2 Pupils reaching expected standards[1]: by gender and age, 1994

England   Percentages

	Teacher assessment		Tests	
	Males	Females	Males	Females
7 year olds[2]				
English				
Handwriting	76	87	76	85
Reading	76	85	76	85
Spelling	67	80	65	77
Writing	64	76	61	74
All elements	75	85	.	.
Mathematics	79	83	.	.
of which: arithmetic	80	84	80	84
Science	85	87	.	.
14 year olds[3]				
English	55	72	49	66
Mathematics	62	67	60	63
Science	63	65	64	63

1 Based on results from responding schools only. See Appendix, Part 3: The National Curriculum: assessments and tests.

2 Percentage of pupils achieving level 2 or above at Key Stage 1.

3 Percentage of pupils achieving level 5 or above at Key Stage 3.

Source: Department for Education and Employment

From: Social Trends 1996, Table 3.4

14.3 Qualifications[1] attained: by gender

England   Percentages

	Males			Females		
	1980/81	1990/91	1993/94	1980/81	1990/91	1993/94
3 or more GCE A levels[2]	10	13	14	8	14	15
1 or more GCE A level[2]	16	21	21	15	23	23
5 or more GCSE grades A-C[3]	24	36	39	26	44	48
1 or more GCSE grades A-C[3]	50	63	64	55	73	75
1 or more GCSE grades A-G[3]	87	95	91	90	95	93

1 Or equivalent.
2 Students at school aged 16 to 18 at start of academic year as a percentage of 17 year old population.
3 Pupils aged 15 at start of academic year as a percentage of the 15 year old school population.

Source: Department for Education and Employment

From: Social Trends 1996, Table 3.6

14.4 Young people reaching NVQ foundation targets[1]: by age

United Kingdom

Percentages

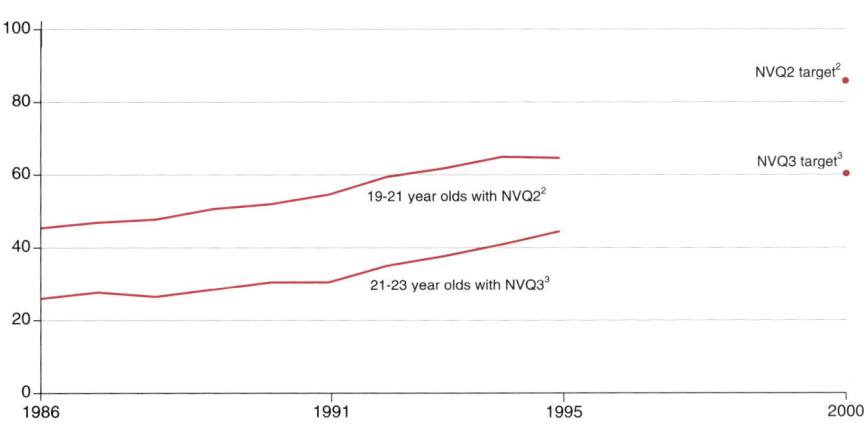

1 At Spring each year.
2 An intermediate GNVQ, an NVQ level 2 or 5 GCSEs grades A to C.
3 An advanced GNVQ, an NVQ level 3 or 2 GCE A levels.

Source: Department for Education and Employment, from the Labour Force Survey

From: Social Trends 1996, Chart 3.9

14.5 School pupils[1]: by type of school[2]

United Kingdom   Thousands

	1970/71	1980/81	1990/91	1993/94	1994/95[3]
Public sector schools[4]					
Nursery[5]	50	89	105	85	86
Primary[5]	5,902	5,171	4,955	5,181	5,251
Secondary					
Modern	1,164	233	94	91	90
Grammar	673	149	156	175	184
Comprehensive	1,313	3,791	2,924	3,033	3,089
Other	403	434	300	288	273
All public sector schools	9,507	9,866	8,533	8,853	8,989
Non-maintained schools					
Pupils aged 10 and under	238	..	266	260	262
Pupils aged 11 and over	383	..	347	342	340
All non-maintained schools	621	619	613	602	602
Special schools[6]	103	148	114	116	116
All schools	10,230	10,633	9,260	9,571	9,707

1 Full-time and part-time pupils are counted as one.
2 Main categories of educational establishments and Stages of education.
3 Data for Wales are for 1993/94.
4 Excludes special schools.
5 Nursery classes within primary schools are included in primary schools except for Scotland in 1990/91
   when they are included in nursery schools.
6 Includes maintained and non-maintained sector.

Source: Department for Education and Employment; Welsh Office; The Scottish Office Education and Industry Department; Department of Education, Northern Ireland

From: Social Trends 1996, Table 3.10

14.6 Average class sizes[1]

Numbers

	One teacher classes						All classes					
	Primary			Secondary			Primary			Secondary		
	1981	1991	1995	1981	1991	1995	1981	1991	1995	1981	1991	1995
Great Britain	..	..	..	..	..	..	..	26.3	26.9	..	19.6	21.5
North	24.1	25.9	26.8	20.5	20.0	21.7	24.7	26.4	27.0	21.2	20.9	22.2
Yorkshire & Humberside	24.7	25.9	27.4	21.3	20.3	21.7	25.1	26.4	27.7	21.9	20.9	22.0
East Midlands	26.0	26.1	27.1	21.2	20.0	21.1	26.3	26.5	27.4	22.0	20.7	21.4
East Anglia	24.5	25.5	25.9	21.0	20.5	20.9	24.9	26.0	26.1	22.2	21.3	21.3
South East	25.0	26.3	27.0	20.5	20.5	21.3	25.3	26.7	27.2	21.1	21.2	21.7
Greater London	23.1	25.8	27.0	19.6	20.6	21.5	23.5	26.2	27.3	20.2	21.2	21.9
Rest of South East	26.2	26.6	27.0	21.1	20.5	21.3	26.6	27.0	27.1	21.8	21.1	21.5
South West	26.1	26.4	27.1	21.7	20.8	21.6	26.4	26.7	27.2	22.2	21.3	21.8
West Midlands	25.1	26.3	27.2	20.8	20.3	21.7	25.4	26.8	27.5	21.3	20.8	22.0
North West	26.0	27.2	27.7	20.7	20.1	21.7	26.2	27.6	27.9	21.4	20.8	21.9
England	25.2	26.3	27.1	20.8	20.3	21.5	25.5	26.8	27.3	21.5	21.0	21.8
Wales	..	..	..	..	19.5	..	..	24.8	25.9	..	21.0	20.2
Scotland	..	..	..	..	..	..	23.8	24.7	24.7	19.9	18.5	19.4

1 Maintained schools only.

Source: Department for Education and Employment; Welsh Office; The Scottish Office Education and Industry Department

From: Regional Trends 1996, Table 4.2

14.7 Enrolments[1] in further and higher education: by type of course

United Kingdom   **Thousands**

	1970/71	1975/76	1980/81	1990/91	1991/92	1992/93	1993/94
Further education							
- Full time[2]	183	318	331	480	550	586	738
- Part time	905	1,423	..	1,759	1,803	1,728	1,756
Higher education							
Undergraduate - Full time	414	464	473	665	748	853	948
- Part time[3]	146	196	248	342	358	456	471
Postgraduate - Full time	43	51	61	84	97	105	116
- Part time[3]	18	23	46	86	98	115	129

1 Home and overseas students. Excludes adult education centres.
2 Data for 1980/81 relate to home students only.
3 Includes Open University.

Source: Department for Education and Employment

From: Social Trends 1996, Table 3.21

14.8 Enrolments in further and higher education: by subject group and gender, 1993/94

United Kingdom   **Thousands**

	Full time		Part time		All enrol-ments[1]
	Males	Females	Males	Females	
Further education					
Combined and general[2]	131	141	200	359	831
Languages/humanities	35	57	111	251	453
Business and finance	60	84	79	206	429
Engineering and technology	76	5	213	18	312
Sciences	33	59	62	94	248
Education	8	6	25	42	81
Social sciences	3	14	10	46	73
All enrolments[3]	360	379	720	1,033	2,494
Higher education					
Combined and general	61	74	8	11	154
Languages/humanities	66	96	10	14	186
Business and finance	77	76	67	64	285
Engineering and technology	124	23	70	8	225
Sciences[4]	145	121	40	111	416
Education[5]	21	58	15	35	128
Social sciences	57	66	15	21	159
All enrolments[6]	550	514	282	319	1,664

1 Includes students in further education in Scotland whose gender is not recorded.
2 Includes GCSE, CSE and GCE courses.
3 Includes enrolments on unspecified courses.
4 Part time includes nursing and paramedic enrolments at Department of Health establishments.
5 Includes teacher training.
6 Part time includes Open University for which there is no subject breakdown.

Source: Department for Education and Employment

From: Social Trends 1996, Table 3.22

14.9 Destination of first degree graduates

United Kingdom   Percentages

	Year of graduation			
	1983[1]	1986[1]	1991	1993
United Kingdom employment[2]	48	53	44	45
Further education or training	21	19	20	21
Believed unemployed	10	7	10	10
Overseas graduates leaving the United Kingdom	4	3	8	10
Not available for employment	2	2		
Overseas employment[3]	2	2	3	2
Destination not known	13	14	13	12
All first degree graduates (=100%)(thousands)	105	112	136	165

1 Data are for Great Britain only.
2 Permanent and temporary.
3 Home students.

Source: Department for Education and Employment

From: Social Trends 1996, Table 3.24

14.10 Average annual public spending per school pupil[1] in real terms[2]: by type of school[3]

Great Britain

£ thousand at 1993-94 prices[2]

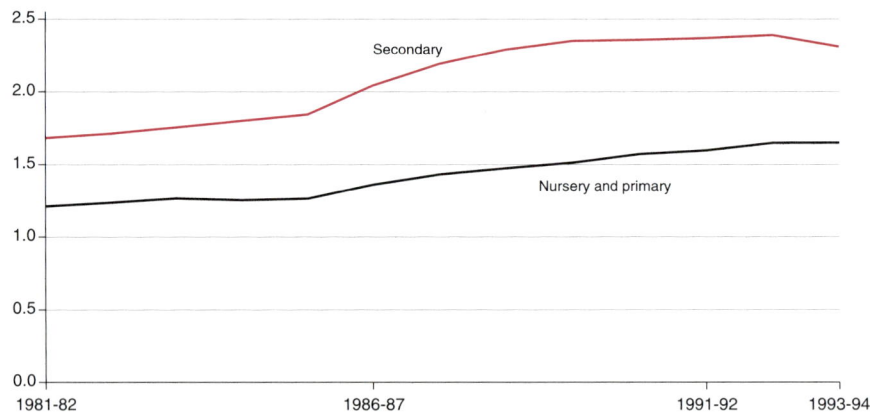

1 Full-time equivalents.
2 Adjusted to 1993-94 prices using the GDP market prices deflator.
3 Excludes grant-maintained schools.

Source: Department for Education and Employment; Welsh Office; The Scottish Office Education and Industry Department

From: Social Trends 1996, Chart 3.27

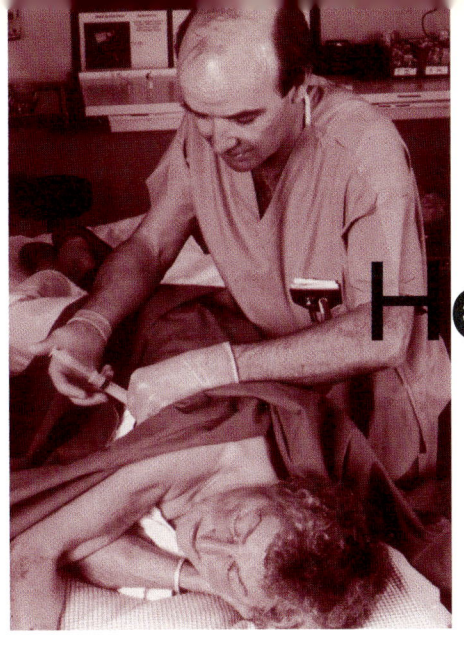

fifteen

Health & personal social services

Definitions and sources

Further health statistics at regional level, including manpower, are given in *Regional Trends*.

For other sources see: *Guide to Official Statistics, 1996 edition* (520 pages approximately, fully indexed) HMSO.

Health and Personal Social Services Statistics for England, HMSO

Social Security Statistics, HMSO

15.1 Expectation of life[1]: by gender and age

United Kingdom								Years
	1901	1931	1961	1991	1994	1996	2001	2021
Males								
At birth	45.5	57.7	67.8	73.2	74.2	74.3	75.2	77.6
At age								
1 year	54.6	62.4	69.5	73.8	74.7	74.8	75.6	77.9
10 years	60.4	65.2	69.9	73.9	74.8	74.9	75.7	78.0
20 years	61.7	66.3	70.3	74.2	75.0	75.1	75.9	78.2
40 years	66.1	69.3	71.4	75.1	75.9	76.0	76.8	78.9
60 years	73.3	74.3	74.9	77.7	78.3	78.4	79.0	80.8
80 years	84.9	84.7	85.2	86.4	86.6	86.6	86.7	87.6
Females								
At birth	49.0	61.6	73.6	78.7	79.4	79.5	80.2	82.6
At age								
1 year	56.8	65.3	75.1	79.2	79.9	79.5	80.5	82.8
10 years	62.7	67.9	75.4	79.4	80.0	80.0	80.6	82.9
20 years	64.1	69.0	75.6	79.5	80.1	80.1	80.8	83.0
40 years	68.3	71.9	76.3	80.0	80.6	80.6	81.2	83.3
60 years	74.6	76.1	78.8	81.9	82.4	82.3	82.8	84.6
80 years	85.3	85.4	86.3	88.3	83.6	88.5	88.6	89.5

1 Total number of years which a person might expect to live.

Source: Government Actuary's Department

From: Social Trends 1996, Table 7.3

15.2 Death rates[1] for people aged under 65: by gender and selected cause of death

United Kingdom

Rates per 100,000 population

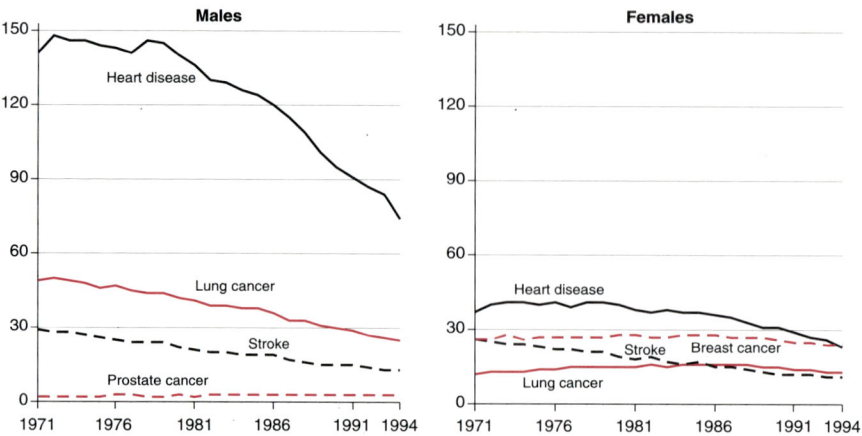

1 Age-standardised to the 1971 population level.

Source: Office for National Statistics; General Register Office (Scotland); General Register Office (Northern Ireland)

From: Social Trends 1996, Chart 7.22

15.3 Percentage[1] of adults who had selected cardiovascular diseases[2]: by gender and age, 1993

England   Percentages

	16-24	25-44	45-64	65-74	75 and over	All aged 16 and over
Males						
High blood pressure	0.3	1.8	10.8	26.5	20.6	8.5
Angina	0.0	0.3	4.0	11.2	7.4	3.1
Diabetes	0.2	1.0	4.3	6.6	8.2	3.0
Abnormal heart rhythm	0.3	1.0	2.7	6.9	5.9	2.4
Heart attack	0.0	0.1	1.0	3.1	2.5	0.9
Stroke	0.0	-	0.3	2.7	4.0	0.7
Heart murmur	0.4	0.4	0.6	1.9	0.2	0.6
Other heart trouble	0.3	0.2	0.7	1.8	1.5	0.6
Females						
High blood pressure	1.0	2.4	13.5	24.1	27.5	10.3
Angina	0.0	0.2	2.3	7.6	11.9	2.7
Abnormal heart rhythm	0.7	1.6	2.6	4.0	3.4	2.2
Diabetes	0.3	0.8	2.6	4.8	4.7	2.1
Heart murmur	0.5	0.9	1.0	0.8	1.0	0.9
Heart attack	0.1	0.1	0.7	1.5	1.3	0.5
Stroke	0.0	0.0	0.4	0.5	1.4	0.3
Other heart trouble	0.1	0.4	0.7	1.4	2.2	0.7

1 Of each age group.
2 Includes related conditions. At the time of interview for blood pressure; in the year before interview for all other conditions.

Source: Health Survey for England, Department of Health

From: Social Trends 1996, Table 7.7

15.4 Consumption[1] of alcohol above sensible[2] levels: by gender and age, 1994-95

Great Britain

Percentages

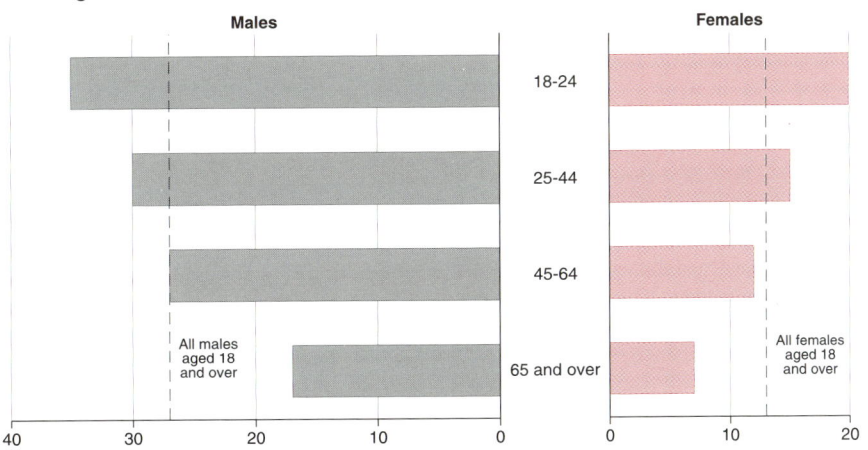

1 By people aged 18 and over.
2 Maximum sensible levels in 1994-95 were 21 units per week for a man and 14 for a woman.

Source: General Household Survey, Office for National Statistics

From: Social Trends 1996, Chart 7.20

15.5 Cigarette smoking[1]: by gender

Great Britain

Percentages

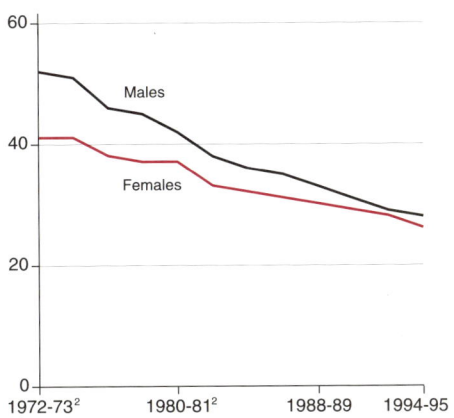

1 By people aged 16 and over, except 1972 which is aged 15 and over. Data are collected every two years.
2 Prior to 1988 data are for calendar years

Source: General Household Survey, Office for National Statistics

From: Social Trends 1996, Chart 7.19

15.6 Breast cancer screening, 1991-92 and 1993-94

United Kingdom		Thousands
	1991-92	1993-94
Invited for screening	1,444	1,609
Screened	1,060	1,209
Cancer detection rates[1]	6.2	5.5
Death rates[2]	46.8	45.2

1 Per 1,000 women screened.
2 Per 100,000 women aged 20 to 74. Death rates for breast cancer.

Source: Department of Health; Office for National Statistics; Welsh Office; National Health Service in Scotland, Common Services Agency; Department of Health and Social Services, Northern Ireland

From: Social Trends 1996, Table 7.15

15.7 AIDS cases and related deaths and reports of HIV-1 infected persons: by probable exposure category and gender, to end June 1995[1]

United Kingdom   Numbers

	AIDS				Reports of HIV-1 infected persons[2]	
	Cases		Related deaths			
	Males	Females	Males	Females	Males	Females
Probable HIV exposure category						
Sexual intercourse						
Between men	8,101	.	5,725	.	15,001	.
Between men and women	782	627	433	333	2,000	2,280
Injecting drug use (IDU)	449	202	292	118	1,885	859
Blood						
Blood factor						
(eg haemophilia)	493	6	424	5	1,218	11
Blood/tissue transfer						
(eg transfusion)	39	71	26	48	77	85
Mother to child	81	82	42	40	152	149
Other/undetermined	100	18	76	9	621	115
All categories	10,045	1,006	7,018	553	20,954	3,499

1 Cumulative reported cases and deaths up to the end of June 1995.
2 Includes 49 reports where the gender was not stated; also includes those individuals who progressed to AIDS.

Source: PHLS Communicable Disease Surveillance Centre

From: Social Trends 1996, Table 7.10

15.8 National Health Service activity for sick and disabled people: out-patients and day cases

Great Britain

	1981	1986	1991-92	1993-94[1]
Out-patient services				
Accident and emergency				
New attendances (thousands)	10,962	12,227	9,859	9,969
Average attendances per new				
patient (numbers)	1.4	1.3	3.5	3.5
Mentally ill				
New attendances (thousands)	230	247	271	301
Average attendances per new				
patient (numbers)	8.8	8.7	7.6	7.2
Mentally handicapped[2]				
New attendances (thousands)	3	4	4	6
Average attendances per new				
patient (numbers)	6.6	9.6	11.5	10.8
Day case attendances (thousands)				
Acute[3]	817	1,208	1,840	2,529
Mentally ill	12	13	1	2
Mentally handicapped[2]	1	4	1	2

1 Data for out-patient services in 1993-94 exclude Wales.
2 Excluding mental handicap community units.
3 Wards for general patients, excluding elderly, younger disabled and neonate cots in maternity units.

Source: Department of Health; Welsh Office; National Health Service in Scotland, Common Services Agency

From: Social Trends 1996, Table 8.13

15.9 Percentage of National Health Service patients waiting[1] over 12 months: by region, 1995[2]

Percentages

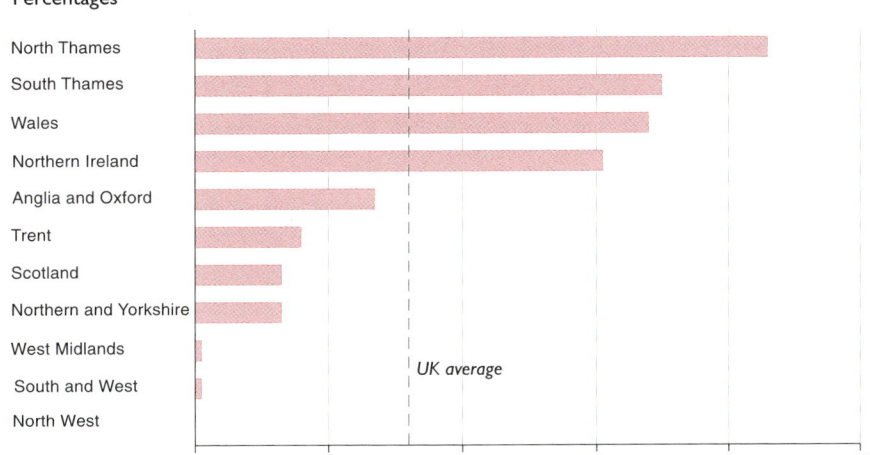

1 All specialties, ordinary (in-patients) and day cases combined.
2 At 31 March.

Source: Department of Health; Welsh Office; National Health Service in Scotland, Common Services Agency; Department of Health and Social Services, Northern Ireland

From: Social Trends 1996, Table 8.14

15.10 Health and personal social services staff[1]

Great Britain				Thousands
	1981	1986	1991	1994
Directly employed National Health Service staff				
Nursing and midwifery [2]	457	472	470	426
Administration and clerical	129	132	152	161
Professional and technical	78	91	103	111
Ancillary and maintenance	238	184	128	108
Medical and dental	48	51	56	60
General/senior managers	.	1	16	26
Ambulance staff	21	22	21	22
Other	7	6	9	4
All health service staff	977	958	954	918
Family health services	27	29	31	32
Family dental services	15	17	18	19
Personal social services	240	270	289	293

1 Whole-time equivalents except family health services and family dental services in Scotland and Wales which are headcounts. Agency and locum staff are excluded.
2 Excludes Project 2000 staff for 1991 and 1994 (in England there were 10.5 thousand and 32 thousand respectively).

Source: Department of Health; Welsh Office; National Health Service in Scotland, Common Services Agency

From: Social Trends 1996, Table 8.8

15.11 Government expenditure on the National Health Service

Years ended 31 March

£ million

	1986 /87	1987 /88	1988 /89	1989 /90	1990 /91	1991 /92	1992 /93	1993 /94	1994 /95
Current expenditure									
Central government:									
Hospitals and Community Health Services[1] and Family Health Services[2]	17 086	18 870	21 110	22 197	25 276	29 061	32 195	35 551	37 674
Administration	553	627	682	855	979	1 119	1 258	-	-
less Payments by patients:									
Hospital services	-99	-106	-347	-407	-510	-540	-505	-368	-376
Pharmaceutical services	-204	-256	-202	-242	-247	-270	-297	-324	-358
Dental services	-261	-290	-282	-340	-441	-477	-470	-440	-434
Ophthalmic services	-1	-1	-	-	-	-	-		
Total	-565	-653	-831	-989	- 1 198	-1 287	-1 272	-1 132	-1 168
Departmental administration	171	193	206	202	268	293	319	270	268
Other central services	577	632	604	693	738	865	1 301	1 631	2 434
Total current expenditure	17 882	19 669	21 771	22 958	26 063	30 051	33 801	36 320	39 208
Capital expenditure									
Central government	1 160	1 212	1 309	2 071	1 848	1 791	1 612	919	619
Total expenditure									
Central government	18 982	20 881	23 080	25 029	27 911	31 842	35 413	37 239	39 827

1 Including the school health service.

2 General Medical Services have been included in the expenditure of the Health Authorities. Therefore, Hospitals and Commumily Health Services and Family Practitioner Services (now Family Health Services) are not identifiable separately.

3 Administration costs are not separately identifiable from 1993/94.

Source: Office for National Statistics

From Annual Abstract of Statistics 1996, Table 3.3

15.12 Children looked after by local authorities[1]: by type of accommodation

England, Wales & Northern Ireland

Percentages

	1981	1993
With foster parents	39	61
In local authority homes	28	13
Placement with parent regulations[2]	19	11
Voluntary homes and hostels	4	2
Schools for children with special educational needs[3]	3	1
Other accommodation	7	14
All children in care (=100%) (thousands)	99	56
All children in care per 1,000 population aged under 18	7.6	4.6

1 At 31 March. All data for Northern Ireland and data for 1981 for England and Wales relate to children in care.

2 All data for Northern Ireland and data for 1981 for England and Wales relate to children under the charge and control of a parent, guardian, relative or friend.

3 England and Wales only.

Source: Department of Health; Welsh Office; Department of Health and Social Services, Northern Ireland

From: Social Trends 1996, Table 8.26

15.13 Health and personal social services for elderly people, 1993-94

England

Rates per 1,000 people aged 65 and over

	1993-94
Hospital in-patients	324
People receiving meals[1]	37
Day centre attendances paid by local authorities[1]	18

1 During survey week in 1994.

Source: Department of Health

From: Social Trends 1996, Table 8.22

sixteen

Housing

Definitions and sources

The main published source of information about housing is the quarterly and annual HMSO publication *Housing and Construction Statistics*. Selected information for individual local authority areas, is shown in *Local Housing Statistics*.

For other sources see: *Guide to Official Statistics, 1996 edition* (520 pages approximately, fully indexed) HMSO.

Census 1991: Housing Topic Report.

Housing and Construction Statistics, HMSO.

Social Trends 1996, HMSO.

16.1   Stock of dwellings[1]: by tenure

United Kingdom

Millions

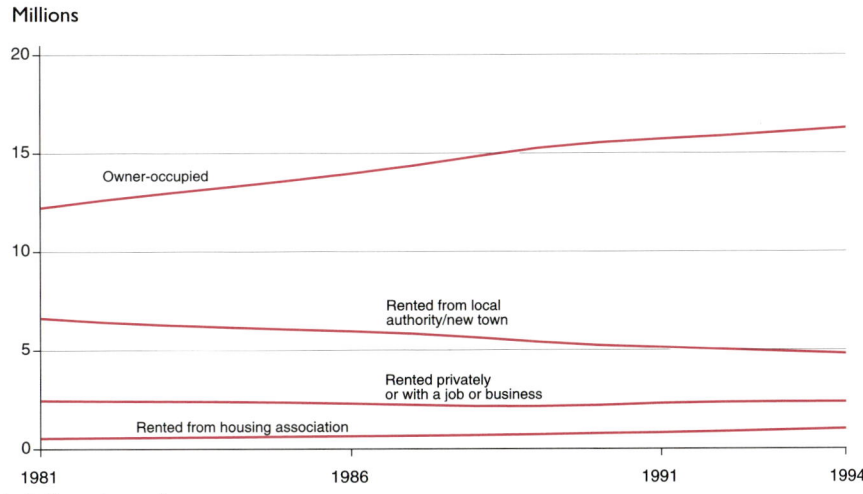

1 At December each year.

Source: Department of the Environment; Welsh Office; The Scottish Office; Department of the Environment, Northern Ireland

From: Social Trends 1996, Chart 10.3

16.2 Indicators of fixed investment in dwellings

	Fixed investment in dwellings (£ million 1990 prices)	Orders received by contractors for new houses (GB) (£ million 1990 prices)	Housing starts (GB)			Housing completions (GB)			Building societies		Quarterly average price of new dwellings at mortgage completion stage
			Private enterprise (thousands)	Housing associations (thousands)	Local authorities new towns and government departments (thousands)	Private enterprise (thousands)	Housing associations (thousands)	Local authorities new towns and government departments (thousands)	Commitments on new dwellings (£ million current prices)	Advances on new dwellings (£ million current prices)	
1989	24 789	7 792	169.9	16.0	15.2	179.6	13.9	17.6	4 377	4 143	..
1990	21 439	5 538	137.0	18.4	8.6	160.7	16.9	16.6	3 779	3 675	..
1991	17 919	5 439	136.8	22.4	4.3	154.1	19.7	10.3	3 903	3 658	..
1992	18 335	5 400	120.1	33.8	2.7	141.1	25.2	4.7	3 230	3 195	..
1993	19 399	6 560	140.9	41.8	2.2	140.5	34.1	2.5	3 139	3 044	73 229
1994	20 149	6 834	156.9	40.8	1.3	146.0	34.3	1.9	4 096	3 875	74 805
1995	19 671	5 649	136.3	32.9	1.2	148.3	38.4	2.0	3 966	3 876	79 274
1991 Q3	4 464	1 409	35.7	5.7	0.9	38.9	5.1	2.5	1 006	923	..
Q4	4 477	1 363	34.6	6.4	0.8	39.2	4.4	1.8	977	952	..
1992 Q1	4 569	1 372	32.0	8.0	0.9	37.4	4.9	1.7	879	855	..
Q2	4 436	1 326	31.3	7.8	0.5	35.5	5.3	1.2	831	835	77 360
Q3	4 560	1 414	29.3	9.5	0.7	36.1	7.0	1.2	771	820	69 893
Q4	4 770	1 288	27.5	8.5	0.6	32.1	8.0	0.6	749	685	70 043
1993 Q1	4 689	1 546	34.8	11.5	0.8	34.7	8.0	0.5	774	764	72 700
Q2	4 876	1 634	34.7	10.4	0.4	34.6	8.5	0.9	776	739	73 289
Q3	4 899	1 647	35.4	9.3	0.7	34.7	8.4	0.6	762	761	73 285
Q4	4 935	1 733	36.0	10.6	0.3	36.5	9.2	0.5	827	780	73 460
1994 Q1	5 239	1 755	38.1	10.8	0.4	33.7	8.7	0.6	967	874	72 892
Q2	5 057	1 773	39.5	11.2	0.3	36.4	7.9	0.4	982	923	74 421
Q3	4 898	1 674	39.9	10.2	0.3	38.5	8.6	0.6	1 095	1 020	74 310
Q4	4 955	1 632	39.4	8.6	0.3	37.4	9.1	0.3	1.052	1 058	76 852
1995 Q1	5 123	1 568	35.8	9.5	0.3	36.8	9.6	0.6	1 006	1 001	74 752
Q2	4 991	1 447	36.0	8.2	0.4	39.3	9.8	0.4	1 054	1 029	78 330
Q3	4 795	1 345	33.4	7.8	0.3	36.7	8.5	0.4	916	919	81 183
Q4	4 762	1 290	31.0	7.6	0.3	36.1	10.7	0.5	990	927	82 388
1996 Q1	..	1 362	32.1	6.8	0.1	36.3	8.6	0.2	969	917	..
1994 Mar	..	592	13.7	3.8	0.1	12.1	3.0	0.1	339	303	..
Apr	..	564	13.3	3.7	0.1	12.1	2.4	0.1	332	301	..
May	..	645	13.2	3.7	0.1	12.3	2.8	0.2	319	297	..
Jun	..	563	13.0	3.8	0.1	11.9	2.7	0.1	331	325	..
Jul	..	562	13.1	3.8	0.1	12.4	2.6	0.3	350	321	..
Aug	..	532	13.4	3.4	0.1	13.3	3.1	0.1	367	335	..
Sep	..	580	13.4	3.0	0.1	12.8	2.9	0.2	378	364	..
Oct	..	535	13.3	3.1	0.1	12.7	2.9	0.1	351	346	..
Nov	..	567	13.1	2.6	0.1	12.6	3.0	0.1	346	353	..
Dec	..	530	13.0	2.9	0.1	12.1	3.2	0.1	355	359	..
1995 Jan	..	468	11.8	3.1	0.1	12.3	3.2	0.2	338	335	..
Feb	..	527	12.3	3.4	0.1	12.9	3.4	0.2	326	324	..
Mar	..	574	11.7	3.0	0.1	11.5	3.0	0.2	342	342	..
Apr	..	473	11.9	2.4	0.2	12.8	3.1	0.2	328	326	..
May	..	484	11.5	2.7	0.1	13.3	3.4	0.1	375	351	..
Jun	..	489	12.7	3.1	0.1	13.0	3.1	0.1	351	352	..
Jul	..	464	11.7	2.3	0.1	12.8	3.0	0.1	312	312	..
Aug	..	455	11.5	2.7	0.1	11.7	2.6	0.1	308	309	..
Sep	..	427	10.0	2.7	0.1	11.6	2.9	0.2	296	298	..
Oct	..	441	10.1	2.8	0.1	11.8	3.4	0.2	326	293	..
Nov	..	441	9.9	2.4	0.1	11.5	3.5	0.2	341	309	..
Dec	..	408	11.1	2.4	0.1	12.3	3.8	0.1	323	325	..
1996 Jan	..	418	10.3	1.9	0.1	13.0	3.0	0.1	322	306	..
Feb	..	446	10.5	2.1	-	11.8	2.6	0.1	322	311	..
Mar	..	497	11.3	2.2	-	11.5	3.0	0	325	300	..

Source: Office for National Statistics; Department of the Environment; Scottish Development Department; Building Societies Association

From: Economic Trends, May 1996, Table 5.5

16.3 Dwelling prices

Indices and £ thousands

| | Index of dwelling prices[1] (1990=100) | | | | | | | | Building society borrowers average dwelling price, 1995 (£ thousands) | | |
									All	Excluding LA sitting tenants	First-time buyers[2]
	1981	1986	1989	1991	1992	1993	1994	1995			
United Kingdom	37	57	101	99	95	93	94	94	63.2	65.1	46.1
North	41	56	88	101	105	107	110	106	46.1	48.4	34.0
Yorkshire & Humberside	37	52	92	104	102	103	100	100	52.6	54.1	39.6
East Midlands	36	53	100	98	96	93	94	93	53.3	54.6	39.9
East Anglia	37	59	112	97	92	88	88	90	59.0	60.5	44.4
South East	..	..	..	..	..	..	..	..	80.0	81.3	58.5
Greater London	33	61	102	96	86	85	89	87	83.5	85.1	64.4
Rest of South East	35	59	109	95	88	84	87	88	78.2	79.4	54.6
South West	37	58	110	97	91	88	89	90	64.0	65.1	47.2
West Midlands	37	49	98	100	97	96	96	96	60.5	62.1	43.3
North West	38	52	87	101	103	99	101	100	55.5	56.4	41.7
England	36	57	102	98	93	90	92	92	65.4	66.9	48.0
Wales	38	53	96	99	98	99	99	98	52.5	53.8	38.6
Scotland	46	66	90	108	113	117	118	116	52.7	58.5	36.4
Northern Ireland	62	82	95	107	109	114	118	131	42.9	45.1	34.2

1 This index adjusts for the mix of dwellings (by size, type, and whether new or second hand) and excludes those bought at non-market prices.
2 Includes LA sitting tenants.

Source: Department of the Environment

From: Regional Trends 1996, Table 6.9

16.4 New mortgages[1]: by gender of borrower

Great Britain

Percentages

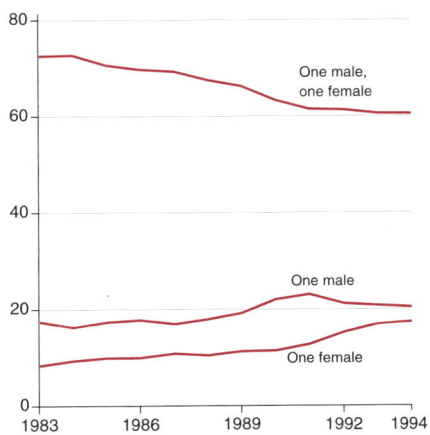

1 New mortgages advanced by building societies, including
Abbey National; sitting tenants are excluded.
Source: Department of the Environment

From: Social Trends 1996, Chart 10.13

16.5 Repossession of properties[1]: warrants issued and executed

England & Wales

Thousands

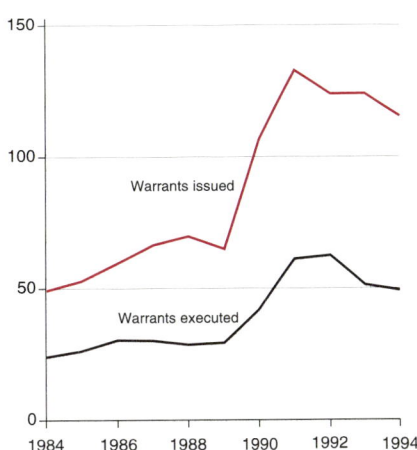

1 Rented and mortgaged.
Source: Lord Chancellor's Department

From: Social Trends 1996, Chart 10.15

16.6 Households: by type of dwelling, 1994-95

Percentages

	Detached house	Semi-detached house	Terraced house	Purpose built flat/ maisonette	Other
United Kingdom	21	32	29	14	5
North	14	40	33	11	2
Yorkshire & Humberside	18	38	33	7	4
East Midlands	28	39	19	11	4
East Anglia	34	38	20	7	2
South East	19	26	29	19	7
Greater London	5	19	36	29	12
Rest of South East	28	31	24	12	4
South West	30	30	22	10	8
West Midlands	23	38	27	10	3
North West	14	41	32	11	2
England	21	34	28	13	5
Wales	23	30	37	7	3
Scotland	15	20	30	32	3
Northern Ireland	29	24	37	7	3

Source: General Household Survey, Office for National Statistics; Continuous Household Survey, Northern Ireland Statistics and Research Agency

From: Regional Trends 1996, Table 6.6

seventeen

Energy

Definitions and sources

All the data shown (except for the chart below) were first published in *Energy Trends* (Monthly).

Detailed definitions and sources are given in the supplementary notes to the *Monthly Digest of Statistics* and in the *Digest of United Kingdom Energy Statistics* (Annual).

For other sources see: *Guide to Official Statistics,* 1996 edition (520 pages approximately, fully indexed) HMSO.

Energy Trends, DTI.

16.1 Inland energy consumption

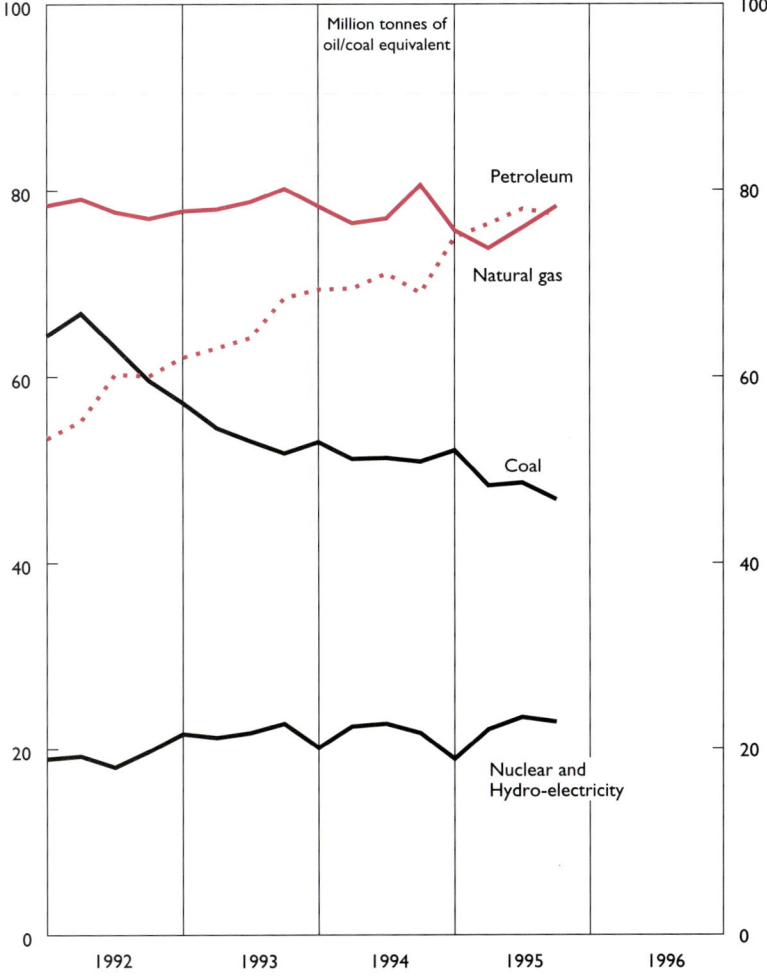

Million tonnes of oil/coal equivalent

Petroleum

Natural gas

Coal

Nuclear and Hydro-electricity

Source: Department of Trade and Industry

From: Economic Trends Chart 5.10

17.2 Inland energy consumption: primary fuel input basis

Million tonnes of oil equivalent

| | Not seasonally adjusted | | | | | | | Seasonally adjusted (annual rates) | | | | | | |
| | | | | Primary electricity | | | | | | | Primary electricity | | | |
	Coal[1]	Petro-leum[2]	Natural gas[3]	Nuclear	Natural flow hydro[5]	Net imports	Total	Coal[1,4]	Petro-leum[2,4]	Natural gas[3,4]	Nuclear	Natural flow hydro[5]	Net imports[6]	Total
1990	67.4	78.3	50.6	16.26	0.45	1.03	214.1	69.2	78.1	56.0	16.26	0.45	1.03	221.0
1991	67.6	77.8	54.1	17.43	0.40	1.41	218.7	67.7	74.8	56.4	17.43	0.40	1.41	218.1
1992	63.6	78.3	55.0	18.45	0.47	1.44	217.2	63.7	78.8	56.4	18.45	0.47	1.44	219.2
1993	55.6	78.9	62.6	21.49	0.39	1.44	220.4	55.6	78.9	63.6	21.49	0.39	1.44	221.4
1994	52.2	77.9	65.2	21.22	0.47	1.45	218.5	53.0	78.9	67.7	21.22	0.47	1.45	222.8
1994 Oct	4.0	5.8	5.30	1.55	0.02	0.12	16.8	51.2	79.10	69.60	20.55	0.37	1.38	222.1
Nov	4.2	6.3	5.50	1.68	0.04	0.12	17.8	50.5	84.80	66.70	22.27	0.67	1.38	226.2
Dec	5.3	7.4	8.50	2.11	0.06	0.14	23.8	5.2	76.80	71.50	20.77	0.51	1.72	223.3
1995 Jan	4.8	5.6	8.50	1.52	0.05	0.11	20.6	56.2	74.60	76.50	17.33	0.49	1.37	226.6
Feb	4.5	6.0	7.60	1.60	0.05	0.11	19.8	52.1	76.90	74.00	19.03	0.52	1.37	224.0
Mar	5.7	7.5	9.00	1.91	0.05	0.13	24.3	53.8	75.10	75.40	18.78	0.39	1.76	225.4
Apr	3.7	5.4	5.60	1.79	0.04	0.11	16.7	50.6	71.60	72.70	23.23	0.37	1.37	219.8
May	3.6	5.4	4.70	1.56	0.02	0.10	15.4	50.4	76.70	77.80	20.56	0.27	1.25	227.0
Jun	4.0	6.9	4.60	1.99	0.02	0.13	17.7	49.8	73.10	80.90	21.71	0.27	1.53	227.4
Jul	3.3	5.5	3.30	1.69	0.01	0.11	14.0	52.8	73.90	82.60	24.74	0.20	1.33	235.0
Aug	3.2	5.6	3.10	1.61	0.01	0.11	13.7	50.8	79.00	74.00	22.72	0.20	1.36	228.1
Sep	3.9	7.0	4.90	2.01	0.02	0.14	18.0	47.0	74.30	78.50	22.17	0.27	1.72	223.9
Oct	3.5	5.7	4.80	1.68	0.03	0.13	15.8	46.5	82.50	73.80	22.39	0.47	1.52	227.1
Nov	3.8	6.2	6.90	1.73	0.03	0.12	18.7	44.3	79.80	75.70	22.99	0.57	1.41	224.7
Dec	5.2	7.4	11.00	2.26	0.03	0.05	25.9	49.5	71.50	83.00	22.22	0.30	0.64	227.1

1 Consumption by fuel producers *plus* disposals (including imports) to final users *plus* (for annual unadjusted figures only) net foreign trade and stock change in other solid fuels.

2 Inland deliveries for energy use *plus* refinery fuel and losses *minus* the differences between deliveries to and actual consumption at power stations and gasworks.

3 Including small amounts of colliery methane, but excluding gas flared or reinjected. Annual data exclude gas used for non-energy purposes.

4 Also temperature corrected.

5 Excludes generation from pumped storage stations. Includes generation at wind stations.

6 Not seasonally adjusted.

Source: Department of Trade and Industry

From: Monthly Digest of Statistics, May 1996, Table 8.1.

17.3 Coal supply and colliery manpower and productivity at BCC mines

	Thousand tonnes						BCC mines			
	Coal supply						Tonnes			
	Production							Average output[4] per manshift worked		
							Wage earners on colliery books (thousands)		Underground	
	Deep-mined	Open cast	Total[1]	Net imports	Imports[2]	Exports[3]		Overall	Total	Produc-tion[5]
1991	73 357	18 636	94 202	17 787	19 611	1 824	49	5.11	6.08	24.66
1992	65 800	18 187	84 493	19 366	20 339	973	35	6.01	7.04	28.90
1993	50 457	17 006	68 199	17 286	18 400	1 114	15	8.03	9.34	40.42
1994	31 854	16 804	48 971	13 817	15 041	1 225	7	11.84	14.22	62.16
1995	35 103	16 369	52 583	15 046	15 871	825	..	..	..	..
1994 Dec	3 101	1 809	4 935	1 132	1 262	129	7[6]	12.9[6]	15.6[6]	73.3[6]
1995 Jan	1 834	826	2 744	1 394	1 466	73	..	..	..	..
Feb	2 901	1 314	4 295	1 059	1 085	25	..	..	..	..
Mar	3 662	1 798	5 550	1 433	1 485	52	..	..	..	..
Apr	2 550	1 183	3 822	1 004	1 071	67	..	..	..	..
May	2 715	1 325	4 146	1 542	1 616	73	..	..	..	..
Jun	3 373	1 665	5 169	950	1 029	79	..	..	..	..
Jul	2 709	1 285	4 102	1 448	1 512	64	..	..	..	..
Aug	2 276	1 186	3 537	1 342	1 396	54	..	..	..	..
Sep	3 689	1 598	5 391	798	890	92	..	..	..	..
Oct	2 687	1 348	4 115	1 637	1 738	101	..	..	..	..
Nov	2 901	1 309	4 287	954	1 035	80	..	..	..	..
Dec	3 808	1 532	5 424	1 485	1 550	65	..	..	..	..

1 Including an estimate for slurry, etc, recovered and disposed of otherwise than by the British Coal Corporation (BCC).

2 As recorded in the *Overseas Trade Statistics of the United Kingdom*.

3 Shipments as recorded by BCC; the figures may differ from those published in OTS.

4 Saleable deep-mined revenue coal.

5 Output from production faces divided by production manshifts.

6 Data no longer available after December 1994.

Source: Department of Trade and Industry

From: Monthly Digest of Statistics, May 1996, Table 8.3.

17.4 Inland use and stocks of coal

Thousand tonnes

	Stocks: end of period				Inland use					
	Fuel producers (consumption)				Final users[5]					
		Secondary				Domestic			Total inland consump-tion	Stocks[8]
	Primary: collieries	Power stations[1]	Coke ovens	Other conversion industries[2]	Industry[3]	House coal[3,4]	Other[6]	Miscell-aneous[7]		
1991	112	83 542	10 011	1 501	6 426	3 150	1 628	1 144	107 513	43 321
1992	79	78 509	9 031	1 319	6 581	2 853	1 303	945	100 620	47 207
1993	48	66 163	8 479	1 329	5 300	2 709	1 930	826	86 783	45 860
1994	22	62 387	8 595	1 190	4 926	1 902	1 974	721	81 717	26 572
1995	8	59 897	8 663	982	4 104	2 923	..	526	77 103	18 043
1994 Dec	2	6 676	831	88	549	152	168[9]	125	8 590	26 572
1995 Jan	1	6 052	679	81	259	172	..	95	7 339	23 916
Feb	-	5 888	657	50	280	145	..	71	7 091	22 008
Mar	-	7 091	842	90	441	212	..	145	8 821	20 224
Apr	1	4 387	670	83	366	155	..	13	5 675	19 140
May	1	4 205	668	80	349	230	..	27	5 560	19 096
Jun	1	4 655	838	89	442	199	..	19	6 244	19 497
Jul	-	3 557	666	76	365	373	..	17	5 055	20 106
Aug	-	3 794	669	70	236	275	..	11	5 055	20 243
Sep	-	4 739	838	72	327	275	..	26	6 277	20 844
Oct	2	4 129	672	92	276	382	..	21	5 573	21 030
Nov	1	4 781	661	98	284	207	..	37	6 068	20 535
Dec	1	6 618	802	103	479	298	..	44	8 344	18 043

1 Coal-fired power stations belonging to major electricity generating companies.
2 Low termperature carbonisation and patent fuel plants.
3 Includes estimated proportion of total imports.
4 Including miners' coal.
5 Disposals by collieries and opencast sites.
6 Anthracite, dry steam coal and imported naturally smokeless fuels.
7 Includes public administration and commerce.
8 Excluding distributed stocks held in merchants' yards, etc, mainly for the domestic market and stocks held by the industrial sector.
9 Included in domestic house coal figure from January 1995 onwards.

Source: Department of Trade and Industry

From: Monthly Digest of Statistics, May 1996, Table 8.4.

17.5 Natural gas production and supply

	GWh				Percentage of net gas available for consumption in the UK		Gas transmitted: GWh[3]
	Gross gas production[1]	Exports	Imports	Gas available[2]	Indigenous	Imported	
1992	597 854	620	61 255	619 286	90.1	9.9	619 921
1993	703 166	6 824	48 528	703 578	93.1	6.9	699.050
1994	750 860	9 557	33 053	724 116	95.4	4.6	724 832
1995	820 831	11 018	19 457	777 376	97.4	2.5	777 483
1995 Jan	100 822	936	2 278	96 893	97.6	2.4	97 211
Feb	83 510	807	1 216	79 472	98.5	1.5	79 572
Mar	89 977	936	2 137	86 293	97.5	2.5	85 931
Apr	67 132	750	1 113	62 225	98.2	1.8	63.457
May	56 480	858	742	51 817	98.6	1.4	52.123
Jun	44 897	560	1 426	42 539	96.6	3.4	41 203
Jul	39 713	882	1 370	35 990	96.2	3.8	36 270
Aug	37 003	956	1 652	33 876	95.1	4.9	34 690
Sep	48 529	810	2 360	46 131	94.9	5.1	43.496
Oct	61 373	1 051	1 147	57 399	98.0	2.0	55 949
Nov	82 894	903	1 913	79 850	97.6	2.4	81 170
Dec	108 501	1 567	2 103	104 893	97.9	2.1	106 361

1 Includes waste and own use for drilling, production and pumping operations but excludes gas flared.
2 Gas available for consumption in the UK. It excludes waste, own use, gas flared and stock change. Includes net imports.
3 Gas input into inland transmission system. Includes public gas supply by North Sea producers, third party supplies, and stock changes. Figures differ from gas available for consumption in the Uk mainly because of stock changes. The figures also differ from total consumption (expressed in oil equivalent in Table 17.2) because they exclude producers' and operators' own use and losses.

Source: Department of Trade and Industry

From: Monthly Digest of Statistics, May 1996, Table 8.5.

17.6 Fuel used by the electricity production and availability from the electricity supply industry[1]

| | Million tonnes of oil equivalent | | | | | Terawatt hours | | | | | | | |
| | Fuel used | | | | | | | Electricity supplied by type of plant | | | | | Total electricity avail able[8] |
	Coal[2]	Oil[2,3]	Nuclear electricity	Hydro-electricity	Total[4]	Electricity generated	Own use[5]	Conventional steam plant[6]	Combined cycle gas turbine	Nuclear	Other[7]	Total	
1991	48.96	5.85	16.30	0.32	71.46	301.49	20.53	217.95	0.31	59.26	3.43	280.96	302.41
1992	45.96	4.96	17.50	0.39	69.83	300.18	20.74	205.90	2.96	66.27	4.31	279.44	301.40
1993	38.26	4.41	20.17	0.30	69.47	300.51	19.34	178.31	22.61	76.84	3.41	281.17	305.20
1994	35.90	3.58	20.05	0.37	69.18	302.81	17.97	167.29	36.82	76.41	4.32	284.84	309.12
1995 Jan	3.46	0.36	1.43	0.05	6.26	27.92	1.58	16.57	3.71	5.46	0.54	26.34	28.21
Feb	3.40	0.34	1.52	0.05	6.15	27.33	1.60	15.85	3.52	5.80	0.56	25.73	27.60
Mar	4.12	0.38	1.82	0.05	7.27	32.61	1.94	19.37	3.77	6.95	0.57	30.67	33.01
Apr	2.53	0.18	1.71	0.04	5.26	23.25	1.38	11.88	3.01	6.53	0.45	21.86	23.66
May	2.40	0.20	1.49	0.02	4.95	22.01	1.29	11.33	3.52	5.67	0.20	20.72	22.40
Jun	2.66	0.21	1.91	0.02	5.74	25.37	1.61	12.11	4.21	7.26	0.18	23.76	25.80
Jul	2.02	0.17	1.62	0.01	4.68	20.52	1.30	9.55	3.40	6.18	0.09	19.22	20.96
Aug	2.16	0.17	1.54	0.01	4.72	20.50	1.31	9.95	3.33	5.85	0.06	19.19	20.94
Sep	2.72	0.24	1.92	0.01	5.89	26.61	1.62	12.95	4.57	7.32	0.15	24.99	27.19
Oct	2.38	0.23	1.61	0.03	5.21	23.30	1.41	11.26	4.17	6.13	0.33	21.90	23.89
Nov	2.74	0.26	1.65	0.03	5.90	26.10	1.50	13.04	4.90	6.28	0.38	24.60	26.44
Dec	3.83	0.37	2.15	0.03	7.80	35.28	2.05	18.22	6.42	8.21	0.39	33.23	34.93

1 Fuel used and electricity generated by major power producers (National Power, PowerGen, Nuclear Electric, National Grid Company, Scottish Power, Hydro-Electric, Scottish Nuclear, NIGEN, Coolkeeragh Power Ltd, Ballyumford Power Ltd, Midlands Electricity, South Western Electricity, Teesside Power Ltd, Lakeland Power Ltd, Fibropower Ltd, Corby Power Ltd, Peterborough Power Ltd, Fibrogen Ltd and Regional Power Ltd) and electricity available through the grid in England and Wales and from distribution companies in Scotland and Northern Ireland.
2 Including quantities used in the production of steam for sale.
3 Including oil used in gas turbine and diesel plant and for lighting up coal-fired boilers and Orimulsion.
4 Including wind power, refuse-derived fuel, natural gas and sour gas.
5 Used in works and for pumping at pumped storage stations.
6 Coal Oil (including Orimulsion) and mixed or dual-fired (including gas).
7 Including gas turbine, diesel, wind and hydro-electric plant.
8 Including net imports and purchases from outside sources mainly UKAEA and British Nuclear Fuels plc, and net of supplies direct from generations to final consumers.

Source: Department of Trade and Industry

From: Monthly Digest of Statistics, May 1996, Table 8.6.

17.7 Sales by the gas and public electricity supply systems

| | Gas: million therms | | | | | | Electricity: Terawatt hours | | | | |
	Electricity generators[1]	Iron and steel industry	Other industries	Domestic	Other[2]	Total	Industrial[3]	Commercial[4]	Domestic	Other[5]	Total
1990	219	462	4 972	10 251	2 998	19 079	98.17	70.96	93.79	8.40	271.32
1991	224	430	5 006	11 395	3 430	20 484	96.87	74.58	98.10	8.20	277.75
1992	611	474	4 674	11 263	3 365	20 409	92.84	77.89	99.48	8.22	278.43
1993	2 790	532	4 658	11 604	3 333	22 919	94.59	79.89	100.46	8.07	283.00
1994	3 909	694	5 249	11 251	3 195	24 275	94.73	80.86	100.64	8.21	284.44
1991 Q3	41	80	967	996	328	2 408	23.48	16.37	17.68	1.91	59.44
Q4	56	100	1 393	3 814	1 073	6 432	24.21	20.27	28.02	2.36	74.86
1992 Q1	91	125	1 354	4 208	1 277	7 040	24.09	21.80	30.71	2.31	78.92
Q2	58	37	1 116	1 867	629	3 707	22.83	17.76	20.64	1.71	62.95
Q3	170	123	860	1 189	339	2 693	22.82	17.52	18.78	1.81	60.94
Q4	291	189	1 344	3 999	1 120	6 969	23.09	20.81	29.35	2.38	75.63
1993 Q1	476	153	1 373	4 262	1 217	7 483	23.82	21.53	30.05	2.02	77.42
Q2	650	123	1 011	1 852	666	4 302	23.06	18.22	21.56	1.69	64.53
Q3	719	115	922	1 268	418	3 442	23.12	18.05	19.09	1.89	62.14
Q4	946	141	1 352	4 222	1 032	7 692	24.60	22.09	29.76	2.48	78.93
1994 Q1	1 043	181	1 519	4 478	1 134	8 356	24.84	21.33	31.31	2.14	79.61
Q2	882	164	1 238	2 148	674	5 106	23.84	19.29	21.06	1.79	65.99
Q3	965	182	989	1 110	468	3 713	22.16	19.13	19.83	1.88	63.00
Q4	1 019	167	1 503	3 515	919	7 100	23.89	21.11	28.45	2.40	75.84
1995 Q1	1 173	199	1 430	4 582	1 370	8 754	25.16	21.81	31.87	2.44	81.29
Q2	1 094	184	1 142	1 871	752	5 043	23.20	19.60	21.13	1.96	65.89
Q3	1 155	105	1 051	1 052	411	3 773	23.03	19.45	19.31	2.00	63.80

1 Power stations belonging to major generating companies, industrial establishments and transport undertakings generating 1 gigawatt or more a year.
2 Public administration, commerce and agriculture.
3 Manufacturing industry, construction, energy and water supply industries.
4 Commercial premises, transport and other service sector consumers.
5 Agriculture, public lighting and combined domestic/commercial premises.

Source: Department of Trade and Industry

From: Monthly Digest of Statistics, May 1996, Table 8.7

Index

A

Abstractions from surface and groundwater 11.6
Aids 15.7
Air pollutants 11.2, 11.3
Airports; passengers 12.9
Alcohol comsumption 15.4

B

Balance of payments
    See chapter 6
Banks 5.2, 5.4
Benefits
    See income
Births;
    EC comparison 7.2
    UK 2.6, 2.7
Breast cancer screening 15.6
British Rail 12.7
Building societies 5.2, 5.4
Burglaries 10.1, 10.3, 10.4, 10.5, 10.6
Buses 12.6
    Passenger traffic EC comparison 7.7

C

Canals; water quality 11.4
Cars 12.1 - 12.5
    Casualties 12.11
    Passenger traffic EC comparison 7.7
Cassettes; trade deliveries 13.5
CD's; trade deliveries; 13.5
Cigarette smoking 15.5
Class sizes 14.6
Clear-up rates for offences 10.5
Coaches; passenger traffic EC comparison 7.7
Coal 17.1 - 17.4
Conceptions 2.5
Consumer credit 5.4, 8.5, 8.6
Consumers' expenditure 8.4
Credit cards 5.4
Crime
    See chapter 10

D

Deaths;
    EC comparison 7.2, 7.5
    Transport death rates 12.12
    UK 2.7, 2.8
Disease;
    Cardiovascular 15.3
    Death rates in EC 7.5
Divorce;
    EC comparison 7.4
    UK 2.10, 2.11
Drug offences 10.3, 10.5, 10.6
Dwellings;
    Fixed investment in 16.2
    Prices 16.3
    Stock of 16.1

E

Earnings 9.3, 9.4, 9.5
Education
    See chapter 14
Electricity 17.1, 17.2, 17.6
Employment
    See chapter 3
    In criminal justice system 10.12
    In health and social services 15.10
Energy
    See chapter 17
Environment
    See chapter 11
Ethnic groups; victims of crime 10.4
European Community
    See chapter 7
Exchange rates 5.3
Expenditure
    See chapter 8

F

Finance
    See chapter 5
Fish stocks 11.5
Fuel production
    See primary fuel production
Further education 14.7, 14.8

G

Gas
    See natural gas
Goods transport; index numbers of 12.4
Graduates 14.9
Gross domestic product
    See chapter 4
Gross national product 4.1 4.2

H

Health
    See chapter 15
Higher education
    See further education
Holidays 13.10, 13.11, 13.12
Household expenditure 8.3
Household income 9.1, 9.8, 9.9
Households;
    Tasks 13.1, 13.2
    Types of dwelling 16.6
    Use of car 12.5
Housing
    See chapter 16

I

Income
    See chapter 9

Index

Index numbers;
    Output 4.6
    Road traffic and goods transport 12.4
Interest rates 5.3
International Labour Organisation 3.5, 3.6
International passenger movements 12.10

L

Labour Force Survey 3.1, 3.2, 3.5 - 3.10
Law
    See chapter 10
Leisure
    See chapter 13
Lending to consumers 8.5
Life expectation 15.1
Literacy 14.1
London Underground 12.7
LP's; trade deliveries 13.5

M

Magazines 13.7
Marriages;
    EC comparison 7.4
    UK 2.9
Monetary aggregates 5.1
Mortgages 16.4
Mothers; economic activity status 3.3
Motoring offences 10.1, 10.2, 10.6

N

National Accounts
    See chapter 4
National Health Service;
    Activity for sick and disabled people 15.8
    Expenditure on 15.11
    Waiting lists 15.9
National Savings 5.4
Natural Gas 17.1, 17.2, 17.5
Newspapers 13.6, 13.7
Nuclear electricity 17.1, 17.2, 17.6
Numeracy 14.1

O

Offences
    See chapter 10
Output; index numbers 4.6
Overseas travel and tourism 13.13

P

Passengers 12.8, 12.9, 12.10
    Death rates 12.12
    Traffic; EC comparison 7.7
Pensioners' income 9.2
Petroleum 17.1, 17.2, 17.7
Physical activities 13.9
Police; complaints against 10.11
Pollutants
    See air pollutants
Population
    See chapter 2
    EC comparison 7.2

Ports; car arrivals and departures 12.8
Prices
    See chapter 8
Primary fuel production 11.7
Prisons 10.8, 10.9
Public sector borrowing requirement 5.2
Pupils;
    Qualifications 14.3
    Public spending per 14.10
    Standards 14.2
    Type of school 14.5

R

Radio listening 13.4
Railways
    See British Rail
    Passenger traffic: EC comparison 7.7
Recycling 11.1
Redundancy 3.10
Regions 1.1, 1.2, 7.1
Repossessions 16.5
Retail Prices Index 8.1
Rivers; water quality 11.4
Road traffic; index numbers 12.5
Robberies 10.1, 10.3, 10.4, 10.5, 10.6

S

Saving 8.7, 8.8
Schools 14.5,
    Class sizes 14.7
Security prices 5.3
Sentences 10.6, 10.7, 10.9, 10.10
Sexual offences 10.1, 10.2, 10.3, 10.5, 10.6
Smoking; see cigarette smoking
Social services
    See chapter 15
Sports 13.9
Supervision orders 10.7

T

Tax and Price Index 8.2
Taxes 9.6, 9.7
Taxis; passenger traffic EC comparison 7.7
Temporary employment 3.8
Theft 10.1, 10.3, 10.4, 10.5, 10.6
Tourism
    See chapter 13
Traffic; index numbers 12.4
Training 3.9
Transport
    See chapter 12
Travel overseas 13.13

U

UK nationals living in other EC states 7.3
Unemployment 3.5, 3.6

W

Wages
    See earnings
Women; in employment 3.3, 3.4

Printed in the United Kingdom for HMSO Dd.0301655, 8/96, 3400, 5673, 356559.